Disaster: God's Warning Bell

If a calamity occurs in a city has not the LORD done it? (Amos 3:6).

"Buy Truth, and do not sell it."
Proverbs 23:23a

Are you aware that sound Bible teaching is a precious and a priceless piece of spiritual jewelry? Indeed, Church History has shown how difficult it is to come by, especially in Christianity today! So when God, from His jewel box of grace, exposes us to pearls of Truth in His infallible and inerrant Word, we ought to embrace and cherish them without reserve. Sound Bible teaching and its application are the treasures that hold our capacity to enjoy abundant life, maximum happiness, friendship, marriage, business, and the source of our unprecedented blessing for today, tomorrow and eternity. Therefore my beloved, "buy Truth" [stay rooted in soundbiblical teaching], for Truth *"...is better than jewels; and all desirable things cannot compare with her [it]"* (Proverbs 8:11).

DISASTER

GOD'S WARNING BELL

MOSES C. ONWUBIKO

Guardian
BOOKS

Belleville, Ontario, Canada

DISASTER: GOD'S WARNING BELL
Copyright © 2009, Moses Onwubiko

All Scripture quotations, unless otherwise specified, are from the *New American Standard Bible*, copyright © The Lockman Foundation 1960, 1962, 1963, 1968, 1971, 1972, 1973. All rights reserved. • Scripture marked KJV, are taken from *The Holy Bible, King James Version.* Copyright © 1977, 1984, Thomas Nelson Inc., Publishers. • Scriptures marked NIV are from *The Holy Bible, New International Version.* Copyright © 1973, 1978, 1984 International Bible Society. Used by permission of Zondervan Publishing House. All rights reserved. • Scripture quotations marked NET are taken from the New English Translation, copyright © 1996–2006 by Biblical Studies Press, L.L.C., www.bible.org. All rights reserved.

Words and phrases in brackets are author's amplifications and not part of the original text.

Library and Archives Canada Cataloguing in Publication

Onwubiko, Moses, 1959-
    Disaster, God's warning bell / Moses Onwubiko.

Includes bibliographies references.
ISBN 978-1-55452-359-7

    1. Disasters--Religious aspects--Christianity. I. Title.
BT161.O58 2009   248.8'6   C2009-900767-3

For more information or
to order additional copies, please contact:

Grace Evangelistic Ministries
P.O. Box 111999 Nashville, TN 37222-1999
www.gemworldwide.org

Guardian Books is an imprint of *Essence Publishing,* a Christian Book Publisher dedicated to furthering the work of Christ through the written word. For more information, contact:
20 Hanna Court, Belleville, Ontario, Canada K8P 5J2
Phone: 1-800-238-6376 • Fax: (613) 962-3055
E-mail: info@essence-publishing.com
Web site: www.essence-publishing.com

Dedicated to my bosom friends:
John G. and Jan Brunner,
whose flaming passion and love for the work of God's Kingdom has become a source of great encouragement to me in every sense of the word!

Table of Contents

Acknowledgments

It goes without saying that a tree by itself cannot make a forest. How true the saying! By the same token, every book, except the Bible, is a composition of one man's inspiration with the contribution of ideas and words of great minds. In view of this, I express my profound gratitude to our team members, Karen Frantzen, Debby Hagar, Richard Hays, John G. Brunner, and the host of our staff members and volunteers for their invaluable contributions. My gratitude also goes to all who are serving our Savior Jesus Christ and fulfilling the "Great Commission" through Grace Evangelistic Ministries. Your partnership, enduring devotion, and relentless support in every sense of the word are indeed yielding huge dividends to the glory of the Almighty God as we are reaching the unreached, coast-to-coast, one person and one nation at a time. Simply put, your commitment and passion for the work of His Kingdom is astronomically beyond human computation! Also, my endless gratitude is poured out without measure to God the Father for His gracious plan of salvation and for the indwelling of His Holy Spirit, the greatest teacher of all time. To crown my overflowing gratitude, my standing ovation goes to no other person than my

Master and Best Friend, King of kings, Lord of lords, the Bright Morning Star—my eternal Lord and Savior Jesus Christ. His unparalleled sacrifice on the cross 2,000 years ago paved the way and made it possible for me—the undeserving one, in every sense of the word—to communicate His infallible Word through this book.

Thanks also to Cindy Thompson, Sherrill Brunton and everyone at Essence Publishing who played a role in the completion of this book.

Moses C. Onwubiko

Word of Hope

> *But a natural [unsaved] man does not accept the things of the Spirit of God; for they are foolishness to him; and he cannot understand them, because they are spiritually apprai*sed (1 Corinthians 2:14).

This is the fact of God's Word! Based on this truth, the information in this book cannot benefit you unless you are a believer in the Lord Jesus Christ. The good news is that you can trust the Lord Jesus Christ for your salvation right this minute, right where you are, and be eternally saved! How good can such good news be? The news even gets better: salvation is a free gift! It is the epitome of God's grace! What's more, it is very simple to obtain. It's as easy as ABC! In Acts of the Apostles 16:30, a man desperate for his eternal destiny asked this urgent question to Paul and Silas: "*Sirs, what must I do to be saved?*" The Scriptures alone provide the one and only answer: "*They [Paul and Silas] said, 'Believe in the Lord Jesus, and you will be saved, you and your household [if they would also believe]'*" (Acts 16:31).

It's that simple! Faith alone in Christ alone!

Elsewhere the apostle John declared, "*But these [facts, including unique miracles that Jesus Christ performed] have been written [recorded] so that you may [have the evidence to] believe that Jesus is the Christ, the Son of God; and that believing [in Christ alone] you may have [eternal] life in His name*" (John 20:31).

Later, the same apostle affirmed, "*Whoever believes that Jesus is the Christ [the Savior] is born of God*" (1 John 5:1).

"*For God so loved the world, that He gave His only begotten Son, that whoever [including you—whoever] believes in Him [will] not perish, but [will] have eternal life*" (John 3:16).

Contrary to public opinion, salvation is not based on morality or good works. It's a free gift (Romans 6:23). The apostle Paul vividly stated, "*For by grace you have been saved through faith; and that not of yourselves, it is the gift of God; not as a result of works [i.e., good works], so that no one may boast*" (Ephesians 2:8-9).

It's faith alone in Christ alone! That's grace! That's God's way! The only way! No other way! Believe on Him and be eternally saved. Right now, you may wish to pause and heed the exhortation of the Holy Spirit: "*For He says, 'AT THE ACCEPTABLE TIME I LISTENED TO YOU, AND ON THE DAY OF SALVATION I HELPED YOU'…behold, now is 'THE DAY OF SALVATION'*" (2 Corinthians 6:2 emphasis added).

You can receive this great and awesome gift of salvation and be forever saved by simply telling God the Father, "God, I am placing my trust entirely on Your Son Jesus Christ as my Savior." The Bible gives the only assurance you need: "*He who believes in the Son has eternal life; but he who does not obey [the command to believe in] the Son will not see life, but the wrath of God abides on him*" (John 3:36).

The moment you believe, you will, for the first time, be

indwelt and filled with the Holy Spirit, who in turn enlightens you as you read on!

Restoration to Fellowship

Sin ruptures our fellowship with God and robs us of the filling of the Holy Spirit, the Greatest Teacher of all time. If you are already a believer in the Lord Jesus Christ, you need to ensure that you are filled with the Holy Spirit, so that He will open your eyes to the truth communicated herein; so you may comprehend and appreciate "*with all the saints what is the breadth and length and height and depth*" (Ephesians 3:18) of His unchanging Word! In preparation, you may pause, search your soul, and acknowledge all known sins to God the Father. The Bible is crystal clear: "*If we confess our [known] sins, He is faithful and righteous to forgive us our [known] sins and to cleanse us from all unrighteousness [unknown or forgotten sins]*" (1 John 1:9).

Dear Heavenly Father,

We approach Your throne of grace with an offering of thanksgiving and petition for all who will be reading this book. We pray that its doctrinal content will be a tremendous source of a challenge and blessing to all of us.

Father, we humbly ask that You revive us in Your truth so that the impact of Your infallible Word will reverberate and reign supreme in our souls. May the content thereof cause people everywhere to take a fresh look at both personal and national disasters. Please challenge us to turn to You in every sense of the word. We lift our prayer in the name of our Savior, Jesus Christ. Amen.

Prologue

The origin of disaster, as to who is behind it, has been widely argued and debated for untold centuries. Our task in this book is to demonstrate through Scriptures that God alone is directly or indirectly behind every disaster, both personal and national. We concede that it will not be an easy task; however we rely solely on the mentorship of the Holy Spirit to aid us in our work. This book is divided into two parts. The first part is dedicated to a panoramic view of God, and the second part is an examination of disasters in relation to the sovereignty of God.

The issue of God's sovereignty in relation to the course of human history will be discussed in detail in part two. Therein it shall be made clear to us that God—not our circumstances—is in control. We shall endeavor to balance the love of God with His justice. In the course of our study, we shall take time to examine individual and national disasters.

God uses calamities as warning bells, except in some cases where He uses them as a means of strengthening His obedient children (James 1:2-4) or as a test, as in the case of Job. We shall discuss these two references later. But other than these, we view every disaster as God's warning bell. It boils down to this: we ought not to explain disasters away. We know that there's no smoke without a fire; similarly, nothing can take place under God's sovereignty without a reason. This is why King Solomon tells us up front: "*In the day of prosperity be happy, But in the day of adversity [disaster] consider [reflect, examine your life]—God has made the one as well as the other*" (Ecclesiastes 7:14).

With this in mind, our objective shall be twofold: first, to demonstrate God's sovereignty over the universe and His awesome control in human history, and second, to explain every human suffering, every disappointment, and every disaster from the viewpoint of Scripture.

Introduction

No doubt about it; we are living in the most interesting time of human history. What a time to be alive! A time when science reigns supreme in human minds! A time when we have become competent in explaining from a scientific viewpoint almost everything that happens under the sun. A time when we are quick in explaining unusual hurricanes, tornadoes, high-powered winds, catastrophic floods, sizzling heat, and bitter cold, just to name a few things from the spectrum of climate changes.

That's not all! It's a time when every one of us has been buried in the grave of economic geniuses who are ever ready to link economic slumps to whatever reason the human mind can fathom. It's a time when government surrounds itself with economic wizards who can interpret economic downtrends in political languages that soothe its political gains. These economic geniuses are quick to pass the buck for the recession from one disastrous incident, such as 9/11, to another. They are quick to pass the buck for high inflation or a high unemployment rate on to the high price for crude oil in the market. They are never hesitant in passing the buck for people losing their homes on to poor management in the housing market. What's more, these wizards never run out of bucks as they toss back and forth the blame for economic woes from one corner to another! That's what government enjoys. Interesting times, indeed!

What more can we say? It's a time when modern medicine has scored high numbers on a scoreboard, a time when men and women in this field waste no time in coming up with theories and medical reasons as to why there's an AIDS epidemic in the world. They are standing by to explain any major disease outbreak with charming medical propositions. What about the problem of the hoof-and-mouth disease in cattle and the Asian flu epidemic? Haven't these been explained medically also? The list can go on and on.

That's right! Scientists are blaming human beings for the catastrophes in the world, claiming that we have caused a great deal by destroying the ozone layers by way of pollution. Electrifying! The economists are passing the blame for recession to any company that is lagging behind in the economic ring. People in the medical field waste no time in explaining away major disease outbreaks. When it comes to analyzing and explaining disastrous circumstances, everyone looks to everywhere and to everything—except to God!

It is alarming that we as believers in the Lord Jesus Christ have joined in. We have joined meteorologists in attributing unusual hurricanes, tornadoes, and floods and every weather-related disaster to so-called Mother Nature. We are scared to death of ascribing any catastrophic disaster to God, who controls history. We reason, "No way; God couldn't do a thing like that." But could He?

Many Bible teachers have been invited again and again on national television to help the rest of the world, the Bible novices, understand why a loving God would allow such a disaster as this or that to take place. These over and over have been given a spotlight to declare the truth concerning God's sovereignty. They have been ushered golden opportunities to set the record straight with regard to equity between God's love and justice—and many of them have come way too short in their representation of the cause of Christianity! Some waffle in their explanations. Others credit disasters to the devil, rather than to God! We ask, "Are believers afraid to call a spade a spade?" Does the Scripture not credit every disaster in a city to God? If the Bible concurs—and it does— why do we refrain from declaring the truth with boldness?

In Amos 3:6, the question was put forth to the skeptics who were having a hard time believing that a loving God could be responsible for a disaster: "*If an alarm sounds in a city, do people not fear?*" Amos asked. He sternly asked another question: "*If disaster overtakes a city, is the LORD not responsible?*" (NET).[1]

Let's read it again, but this time with emphasis: "*If disaster [caused by a hurricane or tornado] overtakes a city, is the LORD not responsible?*" In other words, "Is it not the Lord Himself who brought the disaster to pass?" The question is posed in such a way that it begs for a "yes" answer. Yes, God is responsible! Accordingly, Amos was telling the audience of his day that God is behind every disaster in life! Other writers of the infallible Word of God agreed. In Job 38:22-23, God, during the course of Job's trial, asked him a staggering question: "*Have you entered the storehouses of the snow, Or have you seen the storehouses [armory] of the hail, Which I have reserved for the time of distress [or disaster], For the day of war and battle?*"

---

[1] See also Exodus 4:11.

In Nahum 1:3, the echo is the same: "*The LORD is slow to anger [because He is a gracious God] and great in power, And the LORD will by no means leave the guilty unpunished. In whirlwind and storm is His way [of inflicting disasters], And clouds are the dust beneath His feet.*" Speaking to the Jews in Judah through the prophet Haggai, God declared, "'*I smote you and every work of your hands with blasting wind, mildew and hail; yet you did not come back to Me,' declares the LORD*" (Haggai 2:17). In light of this passage, it's clear that God was responsible for their plight.

That's just a tip of the iceberg. The Psalmist had much more to say on this phenomenal concept. In Psalm 104:4, the writer is emphatic: "*He [God] makes the [devastating] winds His messengers, Flaming fire His ministers.*" You read it correctly. God uses hurricanes and tornadoes as messengers! In light of this, every time these powerful winds pass by us, this passage should remind us that they are God's messengers on a mission. Psalm 119:91 says, "*They stand this day according to Your ordinances, For all things [including floods, tornadoes and hurricanes] are Your servants.*" Also, in Psalm 148:8, we are told that the destroying agents of "*Fire and hail, snow and clouds; Stormy wind, [are in place to fulfill] His word.*" The Psalmist also wrote,

> *Those who go down to the sea in ships [like the Titanic of a century ago], Who do business on great waters; They have seen the works of the LORD, And His wonders in the deep. For He spoke and raised up a stormy wind, Which lifted up the waves of the sea. They rose up to the heavens, they went down to the depths; Their soul melted away in their misery. They reeled and staggered like a drunken man, And were at their wits' end. Then they cried to the LORD in their trouble, And He*

brought them out of their distresses. He caused the storm to be still [majestic sovereignty displayed], So that the waves of the sea were hushed (Psalm 107:23-29).

What a God! The intriguing question is, who is responsible for disasters—in nations or in our lives? Do we hear someone say, "Satan and his minions?" Wrong! Scripture claims otherwise: "*The One forming light and creating darkness, Causing well-being and creating calamity; I am the LORD who does all these*" (Isaiah 45:7). He creates calamities; He manufactures them. That's right! Other passages abound:

Behold, the Lord has a strong and mighty agent; As a storm of hail, a tempest of destruction, Like a storm of mighty overflowing waters, He has cast it down to the earth with His hand (Isaiah 28:2).

Therefore, thus says the Lord GOD, "I will make a violent wind break out in My wrath. There will also be in My anger a flooding rain and hailstones to consume it in wrath" (Ezekiel 13:13).

"*I smote you with scorching wind and mildew; And the caterpillar was devouring Your many gardens and vineyards, fig trees and olive trees; Yet you have not returned to Me,"* declares the LORD (Amos 4:9).

Upon the wicked He will rain snares; Fire and brimstone and burning wind will be the portion of their cup (Psalm 11:6).

Of course, the Bible clearly teaches that God is a God of grace, a God of love, a God who is full of mercy and compassion, and equally, a God of justice. In spite of this, the question we are faced with is not whether God is responsible for disasters. Rather, why should a loving and caring God be involved in devastating destructions? Why did He rain brimstones on Sodom and Gomorrah, which resulted in a total annihilation of its citizens? Why did He destroy the whole earth with the flood in Noah's day? The list of questions can go on indefinitely. The question we should really ask is this: how can a just God *not* rain catastrophic and devastating hail and storms on a nation that sniffs its nose at His justice? *"Upon the wicked He will rain snares; Fire and brimstone and burning wind will be the portion of their cup."* That's what the Bible says. In other words, God is under obligation to hold a chord of love and at the same time strike a balance on a beam of justice.

Think of yourself as a loving and caring parent. How would you handle the issue of your children's total disregard of the rules and regulations in your household? Wouldn't you apply whatever disciplinary measure necessary to deter them from becoming full-blown delinquent children? Would you ignore their bad behavior and look the other way? Think of it. We know that every loving parent would be consumed with finding the right solution. This is why some governments institute laws of capital punishment to send notorious criminals to gas chambers or electric chairs. This is meant to deter heinous crimes. Similarly, God Himself instituted a law of capital punishment for the children of Israel (Deuteronomy 13:10-11).

What would our world be like if we were without laws and law enforcement officers? Who would still be alive if whenever anyone made someone mad, he or she could take the person's life away by murdering the individual, with no consequences for his or her action? Conversely, if we as human beings have in place a system of maintaining law and order, how much more has our omniscient Creator, who in His omniscience knows the right chemistry, the right formula and the right disaster to apply in every circumstance in order to keep chaos in His creation in check? The good news is that God gives us grace first!

He gives us His servants to help us understand His ways and plans for our lives. He reveals to us in His Word the consequences of disobeying His mandates and also the blessings of obedience. My friend, it's only when we rebel against His injunctions that He resorts to the use of disastrous agents as a warning bell to deter us from total collapse. That's justice! God applied this timeless principle to the Southern Kingdom, those of the tribe of Judah, in 606 B.C. Because of their colossal spiritual failure, God sent the Babylonians, who took them into captivity for seventy years. But that was after they drew their last check from the Longsuffering Bank of God. In light of this, Scripture tells us,

> *And the LORD, the God of their fathers, sent word to them again and again by His messengers [that's grace], because He had compassion on His people and on His dwelling place [He does the same today]; but they continually mocked the messengers of God [we are not different today either], despised His words and scoffed at His prophets, until the wrath of the LORD arose against His people, until there was no remedy. Therefore He [God] brought up against them the king of the Chaldeans who slew their young men with the sword in the house of their sanctuary, and had no compassion on young man or virgin, old man or infirm; He gave them all into his hand. All the articles of the house of God, great and small, and the treasures of the*

house of the LORD, and the treasures of the king and of his officers, he brought them all to Babylon. Then they burned the house of God and broke down the wall of Jerusalem, and burned all its fortified buildings with fire and destroyed all its valuable articles (2 Chronicles 36:15-19).

That's God's justice in operation! The passage tells us that God's long-suffering was exhausted. His justice moved Him to action. He judged them! Thomas Jefferson in his *Notes on the State of Virginia* (1781) hit the nail on target when he stormed the crowd with these sobering words: "I tremble for my country when I reflect that God is just; and His justice cannot sleep for ever." Eight years later, George Washington in his inaugural address (1789) said, "The propitious smiles of Heaven can never be expected on a nation that disregards the eternal rules of order and right which Heaven itself [God] has ordained."[2]

On the same wavelength, Billy Graham, an American evangelist lamented, "If God spares America, He will owe Sodom and Gomorrah an apology!" He made the statement based on the fact that Sodom was destroyed because of immorality. Gay and lesbian lifestyles were prevalent in that part of the world. America and a handful of nations are not different today in comparison. It's disheartening, on the one hand, to consider that some churches are giving their blessing nowadays to gay marriages. On the other hand, governmental laws are in place to give these couples equal rights in society. That's not all; immorality in every spectrum in America reigns supreme! Perhaps it was the baking of immorality in the

---

[2] William J. Federer, *America's God and Country* (2000).

American oven that prompted Jefferson in his day to utter those sobering words: "I tremble for my country when I reflect that God is just; and His justice cannot sleep for ever." He may have been thinking about this passage:

But if you do not obey Me and do not carry out all these commandments, if, instead, you reject My statutes, and if your soul abhors My ordinances so as not to carry out all My commandments, and so break My covenant, I, in turn, will do this to you: I will appoint over you a sudden terror, consumption and fever that will waste away the eyes and cause the soul to pine away; also, you will sow your seed uselessly, for your enemies will eat it up. And I will set My face against you so that you shall be struck down before your enemies; and those who hate you shall rule over you, and you shall flee when no one is pursuing you. I will set My face against you so that you will be struck down before your enemies; and those who hate you will rule over you, and you will flee when no one is pursuing you (Leviticus 26:14-17).

God's justice cannot sleep forever! God warned that if we should ignore His injunctions, He would send us terror: "*I [God] will appoint over you a sudden terror.*" Sounds familiar? Does 9/11 ring a bell? We wonder who in his right mind could allow the terrorists to hit America hard. Scripture leaves us no room for wondering! The souls of the inhabitants of the United States of America continue to pine away on account of terrorism. God keeps His Word!

Additionally, He said that we shall flee when no one is pursuing us. Sound familiar too? We recall that following the incidents of 9/11, many people in America were running to stores buying duct tape and gas masks in preparation for a gas attack when no one was really pursuing them with gas or biological agents! But that's exactly what Scripture says will happen to a nation if it fails to recognize the supremacy of Heaven or will happen to anyone who disregards the eternal rules of order and right which Heaven itself (God) has ordained. What about economic depression? God warns us, according to the words of the prophet Ezekiel:

> *Then the word of the LORD came to me saying, "Son of man, if a country sins against Me by committing unfaithfulness, and I stretch out My hand against it, destroy its supply of bread [agricultural economy], send famine [severe recession] against it and cut off from it both man and beast, even though these three men, Noah, Daniel, and Job [the faithful ones] were in its midst, by their own righteousness they could only deliver themselves," declares the Lord GOD* (Ezekiel 14:12-14).

My friend, if you have been following this introduction objectively, it will be unreasonable for you to still blame one political party or another for economic depression. How can anyone who accepts the Bible as the inerrant Word of God read all the Bible passages quoted and still attribute Katrina to Mother Nature? Having accepted these biblical truths, my friend, there's no reason why we should blame the ozone layer depletion for the extraordinary changes in our weather pattern. God is sovereign! *"He [God] makes the [devastating] winds His messengers, Flaming fire His ministers"* (Psalm 104:4).

After this detailed introduction, we can hardly wait to get into part one and lay the foundation of our work.

Arguably, this section is the backbone that holds the skeletal structure of this book. In view of this, we shall, in this section, take time to examine God, His Person, sovereignty, and integrity and see how the God of the universe controls the affairs of man. Simply stated, we cannot properly relate to disaster apart from a measure of understanding of who and what God is! Who is God?

PART I | The Panoramic View of God

Arguably, this section is the backbone that holds the skeletal structure of this book. In view of this, we shall, in this section, spend reasonable time to examine God, His Person, sovereignty, integrity and see how the God of universe inter-relates with the affairs of man. Simply stated, we cannot properly relate to disaster apart from a measure of understanding of Who and What God is! Who is God?

1 | Comprehending the True God

Know therefore today, and take it to your heart, that the LORD, He is God in heaven above and on the earth below; there is no other (Deuteronomy 4:39).

For You are the LORD Most High over all the earth; You are exalted far above all gods (Psalm 97:9).

Foundational to our entire work is who and what the true God is. Because of this, we have set aside three chapters to examine the subject of God.

Common sense will tell us that how one perceives equipment will affect one's attitude toward it. Take two grinding machines, for example. If you know that one of the machines is so incredibly powerful that it can chop and grind a whole cow's flesh and bones in a matter of seconds, while the other is so dull that it can hardly chop a tomato, let alone a finger, your attitude toward those machines will differ accordingly. You will undoubtedly approach the first machine with more caution than the second.

This is true in spiritual life! Our attitude toward the God of the universe is directly proportional to how we perceive Him. If we perceive Him as a created being, we will approach

Him as we would other creatures. If we perceive Him as a god who manifests Himself through objects, we will approach Him through idolatry. If we perceive Him to be just another powerful higher being roaming around out there in space, we will approach Him as if there are other higher beings besides Him. On the other hand, if we perceive Him to be an infinite, omnipotent, and sovereign being, we will approach Him as the only God of the universe, with great awe and reverence.

While many of us have varied perceptions of God, the only true perception is that derived from Scripture. All other perceptions end in idolatry! This raises a question: who is God? We shall answer this question as this study progresses.

I have asked that question a thousand and one times to a thousand and one people around the world as I travel with the good news of Jesus Christ. The answer varies, depending on the people and their culture. For example, one of the countries I visited has over 33 million gods and goddesses. Consequently, their definition of God can be summed up in one word: *confusion*. What was heartbreaking was hearing some of the definitions from Christians in the same locale who had just embraced Christianity. That is not surprising, of course, considering that their perception of God until then had been influenced by an idolatrous culture. Accordingly, every religion other than Christianity has its unique definition of God, all of which differ from the God of the Bible. What is chilling is that even in the Christian community the perception and definition of God sharply differ from one denomination to another! We reiterate: our attitude toward the God of the universe is directly proportional to our understanding of who He really is. By the same token, it affects how we worship Him!

This brings us to another question: namely, what bearing has our comprehension of God on our explanation of disasters? The bearing is profound! Ironically, those who ascribe disasters to Mother Nature are likely to be those who view God as a being disconnected from what is going on in the world, though supreme. On the other hand, those who deny God's involvement in disaster probably perceive Him as a being who manifests nothing but love all day long. That leaves those who accept the fact that everything that happens under the sun does so under the sovereign directive, super-intendence, and control of the Almighty God. They view everything, including disaster, from the binoculars of the infallible Word of God. They perceive God to be an infinite, omnipotent, and sovereign Being who directs and controls all events of human history. We shall discuss God's sovereignty in detail when we get to chapter 3. We are back to the real question of this chapter: who is God?

Let there be no misunderstanding! Our goal for this book is not to present an elaborate teaching about God. Rather, our objective is simply to demonstrate God's sovereignty over the universe and His awesome control in human his-tory, including disasters. In a nutshell, God is the Creator of the whole universe, and He Himself was not created. On this bedrock rest the building blocks of this chapter. God exists! What we know about the true God we know from the infal-lible Word of God, namely, the Bible! One may ask, "Can the Bible be trusted?" To answer this question, we would like to briefly mention a few facts about the Bible.

THE UNIQUENESS OF THE BIBLE

The good news is that God in His infinite grace found a way to reveal Himself to us. The work of His hand is one avenue of His revelation. He spoke to us through His angelic beings. He spoke through prophets like Moses, Isaiah,

Jeremiah, Ezekiel, and others as well as through visions and dreams. People heard His voice! No one can make that claim for any god other than the God of the universe. Above all, we have the final revelation of Him through His Son Jesus Christ, who said to His disciples that He is the true representation of God the Father (John 14:9; cf. 10:30). God's Word to these on record is what we now call the Holy Bible, a book that was written by approximately forty authors in a timeframe of 1,500 years or so.

The Bible is the guiding light of civilization and liberty, the oldest book in existence. More than that, it has withstood every storm for three millennia and counting. Countless efforts have been made to banish it from the face of the earth. People have hidden it and burned it (Jeremiah 36:20-23), and God replaced it (vv. 27-32)! Some governments have made possession of it a crime punishable by death, and the most bitter and relentless persecution has been waged against those who had faith in it. Guess what? The Bible is still alive (Hebrews 4:12)! The fact that this book has survived so many centuries despite such unparalleled efforts to banish and destroy it is circumstantial evidence that the Great Being, God, whom it claims as its Author, has also been its preserver! We can rely on its claims!

That's not all! It's intriguing is that the authors of the Bible never had a round-table discussion, never compared notes with one another, and yet their work has no contradictions whatsoever! Amazing, is it not? That's because the God of the Bible is an amazing God! In no other book can we find such coherency of thought and fulfilled prophecy. It's from this book that we know what we know about the true God; and it's from it that we would, with great reverence, briefly discuss the doctrine of God.

Nowhere in the entire Bible does Scripture ever attempt to prove God's existence. It assumes that God exists; and He does! On the other hand, it calls those who do not accept this phenomenal revelation "fools." "*The fool has said in his heart, 'There is no God.' They are corrupt, they have committed abominable deeds; there is no one who does good*'" (Psalm 14:1). They are corrupt! That sums up the reasons for their rejection of a Supreme Being, as corrupt minds are incapable of perceiving truths or realities.

At this juncture, we consider it of paramount importance to drive the words of the Psalmist home with an illustration. Imagine a situation where every living thing except two intelligent babies who never saw their caregiver is removed from the planet Earth in such a way that these two never discover any traces of life that pre-existed them. Practically, all other things remain unchanged. These two grow up to adulthood and begin to move around from place to place. As they move around, they see things such as freeways, highways, parked automobiles, airports, and airplanes, just to name a few, and realize that these were systematically designed and orderly arranged. One day, they decide to explore the cockpit of an airplane. Entering, they find themselves breathless because of how sophisticated the plane is designed. Seeing all this, my friend, they would be dead fools to walk out of that cockpit and immediately come to the conclusion that everything around them in all its glory must be accidental. Rather, one would expect them to come to some kind of conclusion that someone, perhaps a higher being superior in knowledge with a sophisticated mind, must have brought everything around them into existence. That's why the Psalmist wasted no time in indicting one who refuses to realize that every system must call for a designer.

"The heavens are telling of the glory of God; And their expanse is declaring the work of His hands" (Psalm 19:1). And the apostle Paul confirmed,

> *For the wrath of God is revealed from heaven against all ungodliness and unrighteousness of men who suppress the truth in unrighteousness, because that which is known about God is evident within them; for God made it evident to them. For since the creation of the world His invisible attributes, His eternal power and divine nature, have been clearly seen, being understood through [the sophistication of] what has been made, so that they are without excuse. For even though they knew God, they did not honor Him as God or give thanks, but they became futile in their speculations [of evolution and what not], and their foolish heart was darkened. Professing to be wise, they became fools* (Romans 1:18-22).

Rightly so, we shall begin where the Bible began: *"In the beginning God created the heavens and the earth"* (Genesis 1:1).

GOD THE CREATOR

> *"The heavens are telling of the glory of God; and their expanse is declaring the work of His hands"* (Psalm 19:1).

I always hold my breath in amazement when I walk past the cockpit of an airplane. Twice I have had the opportunity to have a pilot explain to me the function of some of those sophisticated buttons. What a feast for my inquisitive mind! I often ask how in the world a plane can take off into the air, flying to an altitude of 30,000 to 40,000 feet with such a weight of people and goods. That's not even the end of my bafflement! How can it take off from a country like the United States of America and fly into the interior of Africa or Asia without getting lost? Amazing, is it not? I know that all this can be explained in relation to physics, aerodynamics, and the like. The truth of the matter is that no amount of explanation can totally extinguish the fire of my amazement. Looking back, it's the fruit of the labor of two geniuses, Orville and Wilbur Wright. In 1903, these brothers stormed the world by inventing the first airplane. They created the airplane in history!

Think of it! A higher being must have endowed them with ingenuity. That notwithstanding, the idea to build an airplane was first conceived in their minds and one day hatched into action when they actually built and then tested a finished product. In relation to their work, we can say that they pre-existed and are sovereign over the work of their hands. In light of this, when they were manufacturing the aircraft, they had access to the plane, inside and out. They had total control. That's sovereignty! That goes for whatever man makes. What man makes, man controls!

God, the Creator, pre-existed all things. He created the universe and everything therein, including the Wright brothers! This implies that God is not bound by the universe, which He created. He is an infinite Being, and we are finite beings. He created us! Like an aircraft manufacturer, God created everything we see, both animate and inanimate things. He created them all, for a purpose that He hid within Himself. That's why we must revere Him. That's why God called for His creatures to glorify Him by means of worship (Isaiah 43:7).

Common sense tells us that it does not make sense to praise and worship a product rather than the manufacturer itself. Well, that's exactly what we do when we worship any object that God created. We make fools of ourselves when we worship objects other than the one who made them! Creatures worshipping creatures rather than the Creator makes absolutely no sense whatsoever! This is why God strongly opposes all forms of idolatry. We shall examine this later in our study. But first, let's define God. We concede that with our finite minds, it will be very difficult to competently define a God with such creative and awesome power. To really get our point across, let's consider God's dialogue with Job:

"Where were you when I laid the earth's foundation? Tell me, if you understand. Who marked off its dimensions? Surely you know! stretched a measuring line across it? On what were its footings set, or who laid its cornerstone—while the morning stars sang together and all the angels shouted for joy? Who shut up the sea behind doors when it burst forth from the womb, when I made the clouds its garment and wrapped it in thick darkness, when I fixed limits for it and set its doors and bars in place, when I said, 'This far you may come and no farther; here is where your proud waves halt'? Have you ever given orders to the morning, or shown the dawn its place, that it might take the earth by the edges and shake the wicked out of it? The earth takes shape like clay under a seal; its features stand out like those of a garment. The wicked are denied their light, and their upraised arm is broken. Have you journeyed to the springs of the sea or walked in the recesses of the deep?

Have the gates of death been shown to you? Have you seen the gates of the shadow of death? Have you comprehended the vast expanses of the earth? Tell me, if you know all this. What is the way to the abode of light? And where does darkness reside? Can you take them to their places? Do you know the paths to their dwellings? Surely you know, for you were already born! You have lived so many years! Have you entered the storehouses of the snow or seen the storehouses of the hail, which I reserve for times of trouble, for days of war and battle? What is the way to the place where the lightning is dispersed, or the place where the east winds are scattered over the earth? Who cuts a channel for the torrents of rain, and a path for the thunderstorm, to water a land where no man lives, a desert with no one in it, to satisfy a desolate wasteland and make it sprout with grass? Does the rain have a father? Who fathers the drops of dew? From whose womb comes the ice? Who gives birth to the frost from the heavens when the waters become hard as stone, when the surface of the deep is frozen? Can you bind the beautiful Pleiades? Can you loose the cords of Orion? Can you bring forth the constellations in their seasons or lead out the Bear with its cubs? Do you know the laws of the heavens? Can you set up God's dominion over the earth? Can you raise your voice to the clouds and cover yourself with a flood of water? Do you send the lightning bolts on their way? Do they report to you, 'Here we are'? Who endowed the heart with wisdom gave understanding to the mind? Who has the wisdom to count the clouds? Who can tip over the water jars of the heavens when the dust becomes hard and the clods of earth stick together? Do you hunt the prey for the lioness and satisfy the hunger of the lions when they crouch in their dens or lie in wait in a thicket? Who provides food for the raven when its young cry out to God and wander about for lack of food? Do you know when the mountain goats give birth? Do you watch when the doe bears her fawn? Do you count the months till they bear? Do you know the time they give birth? They crouch down and bring forth their young; their labor pains are ended. Their young thrive and grow strong in the wilds; they leave and do not return" (Job 38:4-29, NIV).

Now that we have feasted our minds on God's amazing creation, we can step out and with reverence define the God of universe.

GOD DEFINED

God is an invisible, personal, and living spirit, distinguished from all other spirits by several kinds of attributes: metaphysically, God is self-existent, eternal and unchanging; intellectually God is omniscient [all knowing], faithful, and wise; ethically God is just, merciful, and loving; emotionally, God detests evil, is long suffering, and is compassionate; existentially, God is free, authentic, and omnipotent [all powerful]; relationally, God is transcendent in being, immanent universally in providential activity, and immanent with his people in redemptive activity.[3]

This definition, as we can see, can go on and on infinitely!

---

[3] Gordon R. Lewis, "God, Attributes of," in Walter A. Elwell, ed., *Evangelical Dictionary of Theology* (Grand Rapids: Baker, 1984), p. 541.

Westminster offered a somewhat concise definition: "God is a Spirit, infinite, eternal, and unchangeable, in his being, wisdom, power, holiness, justice, goodness, and truth."[4]

In light of these definitions, you can see why we said previously that defining God is no ordinary task, for no finite being is capable of giving a comprehensive and concise definition of an infinite Being. God of the universe is way too big to be squeezed in one paragraph of definition by finite little tiny creatures like us. Simply, God is *One*, eternal, immutable, truthful, righteous, omniscient, omnipotent, omnipresence, and sovereign, who possesses the attributes of a person with neither beginning nor ending, who manifests Himself in three distinct personalities and functions.

The sublime truth is that God is *bigger* than any definition man can come up with! He is totally incomprehensible! How can we define a God who sees everything, knows everything, hears every language, and simultaneously controls everything? What an awesome God! This clears the way to examine yet another crucial biblical teaching: the Godhead.

THE PERSONS OF THE GODHEAD

The biblical teaching of the Godhead or Trinity makes a sharp demarcation between Christianity and religion. Of course Christianity is not a religion. A religion in a more expounded definition is nothing but man's total disregard of God's only provision of redemption through the person and the work of Jesus Christ. Simply, it's man seeking to gain God's favor through man's good deeds. Religion is the

_____

4 *Westminster Shorter Catechism* (Q. 4).

devil's wildcard![5] The true God of the Bible abhors religion in all its ugliness. Some ministers of the gospel have occasionally been asked on national television, "Would anyone other than a Christian go to Heaven?" This is a straightforward question that requires a straightforward answer; but unfortunately those I have seen wavered and waffled in their answers. In contrast, when the apostle Paul faced off with the religious crowd of the Jewish nation, he did not shrink; he did not waffle; he did not waver from declaring them to be a lost people. In Romans we read,

> *"Brethren, my heart's desire and my prayer to God for them [the Jews] is for their salvation [because many are yet to be saved]. For I testify about them that they have a zeal for God [like every religious group does], but not in accordance with knowledge [of what God requires for salvation]. For not knowing about God's righteousness [a requirement for a relationship with God] and seeking to establish their own [through their own good deeds—religion], they did not subject themselves to the righteousness of God [which is by faith alone in Christ alone]"* (Romans 10:1-3; cf. 9:30-33).

Simply put, one's attitude toward the Person and the work of Jesus Christ will determine whether one will spend eternity with God in Heaven or in Hell, separated from God for all eternity. The eternal repercussions of rejection of Christ is sobering; that's why we want to incorporate this section into our study in relation to the issue of the Godhead.

---

[5] Moses C. Onwubiko, *Humility, the Epitome of Christian Living.*

We know from Scripture that the Jews throughout their history were acutely aware of the oneness of God: "*Hear, O Israel! The LORD is our God, the LORD is one!*" (Deuteronomy 6:4). On the other hand, we should bear in mind that God did not reveal Himself to man all at once. He did it bit by bit—progressively. This progressive revelation came to a screeching halt in the book of Revelation (Revelation 22:18). For instance, God in His infinite wisdom did not reveal Himself and His plan in total to Adam and Eve; otherwise they probably would not have disobeyed God, knowing the eternal ramifications of their disobedience. Similarly, God did not unveil Himself completely to Abraham; neither did He to Moses, who, when the Lord sent him on a mission to Egypt,

> *said to God, "Behold, I am going to the sons of Israel, and I will say to them, 'The God of your fathers has sent me to you.' Now they may say to me, 'What is His name?' What shall I say to them?" God said to Moses, "I AM WHO I AM"; and He said, "Thus you shall say to the sons of Israel, 'I AM has sent me to you'"* (Exodus 3:13-14).

Who would ever have thought then that the "I AM" that came to Moses was actually the Son of God (John 8:58)?

Not until the New Testament and the incarnation of Jesus Christ did God's revelation came to fruition to the extent that He chose to reveal Himself to man. When the Lord's ministry ended, after He had paid for the sins of the entire human race and ascended back to Heaven from whence He came (John 6:38), the apostles, especially Paul, went to work interweaving together both the Old and New Testament rev-

45

elation. It was there and then that they knew what we know today about the awesome God of the universe. After the apostolic teachings, it became clear that Jesus Christ is equally God (John 1:1; Philippians 2:6-8; Hebrews 1:2-3, 8-12; Colossians 1:15, 19, 2:9). The Jewish people had known for ages that God is One; but not until the incarnate state of Jesus Christ did it become fully apparent that though One God, He exists in three personalities. This startling revelation ultimately led to the theological coinage of our famous word *Trinity*.

But again, the word *Trinity* has been a bone of contention for centuries, even among Christians. I wonder how one can call oneself a Christian and reject the biblical teaching of the Trinity, which is vividly revealed in the New Testament. Frankly, the subject has caused many religious groups to shy away from embracing Christianity while alleging that Christians worship three gods! But do Christians worship three gods? No, not at all! Worshipping three gods would be tantamount to idolatry!

It will be even more challenging to define the Trinity than to define the infinite God of the universe. First it requires two things, that we have trusted in the Lord Jesus Christ and that we accept the Bible as the totally infallible, inerrant, and authoritative Word of God.

TRINITY DEFINED

God is One, who, without a beginning, in eternity past elected to manifest Himself in three distinct personalities, three distinct fuctions, with each Person having identical essence, co-eternal, co-equal, and co-infinite with perfect harmony.

B.B. Warfield defined *Trinity* more concisely: "There is one only and true God, but in the unity of the Godhead there are three coeternal and coequal persons, the same in substance but distinct in subsistence (existence)."[6]

The Bible reveals the first person in the Godhead as the Father, the second as the Son, and the third as the Holy Spirit. *Father* is used here not in the natural sense of parenthood as some religious people thought. Rather He is designated as a father in the same manner as an earthly father assumes the authority in a household. The Father and the Holy Spirit are the invisible members of the Trinity. "*God [the Father] is spirit, and those who worship Him must worship in spirit and truth*" (John 4:24). And as for the third member, the Holy Spirit, He is Spirit by virtue of His name. The second member is the Son, the only visible member of the Godhead. He is called the Son in relation to service, not because He was physically born of the Father. In relation to the Father, Jesus Christ Himself, recognizing His authority, said, "*For I have come down from heaven, not to do My own will, but the will of Him who sent Me*" (John 6:38; cf. 4:34; 5:19, 30; Hebrews 10:7). In relation to Jesus' functions, Scriptures abound, for He is the Creator and the One whom the Father offered as a Sin Offering for the entire human race:

> *In the beginning [eternity past] was the Word, and the Word was with God, and the Word was God [the Son, co-eternal, co-equal and co-infinite with God the Father]...All things came into being through Him, and apart from Him nothing came into being that has come into being* (John 1:1-3).

_____

6 B. B. Warfield, "Trinity," *The International Standard Bible Encyclopedia*, James Orr, ed. (Grand Rapids: Eerdmans, 1930), 5:3012.

For by Him all things were created, both in the heavens and on earth, visible and invisible, whether thrones or dominions or rulers or authorities—all things have been created through Him and for Him (Colossians 1:16).

"*But God demonstrates His own love toward us, in that while we were yet sinners, Christ died for us*" (Romans 5:8; cf. 2 Corinthians 5:21; Romans 3:25; 8:3). He is the only One whom the Father appointed as an offering for our sins and the only means of salvation. That's why the apostle Peter was so emphatic in declaring: "*And there is salvation in no one else; for there is no other name under heaven that has been given among men by which we must be saved*" (Acts 4:12).

This equally explains why Christians maintain that everyone who rejects Jesus Christ as the Savior will be damned forever. That may sound too extreme, too narrow-minded, but my friend, it's a matter of life and death! John the Baptist said, "*He who believes in the Son has eternal life; but he who does not obey [who refuses to believe on] the Son will not see life, but the wrath of God abides on him*" (John 3:36). Jesus Christ Himself affirmed that, as recorded in John 8:24, "*Therefore I said to you that you will die in your sins; for unless you believe that I am He [God the Son, the Savior], you will die in your sins,*" and in John 14:6, "*I am the way, and the truth, and the life; no one comes to the Father [in Heaven] but through Me.*'" How much more emphatic can He be?

An important question a religious man may ask is "If Christians don't worship three Gods as declared previously, why is it that each member is called God?"

That's a very good question! In fact, theologians have used many illustrations in attempting to answer this mind-stimulating question. We concede that no one had come up with a perfect illustration yet, and perhaps no one will. Keep in mind that every time a finite creature is laboring to explain an infinite Being beyond what Scripture reveals, the creature, no matter how ingenious he may be, would always come short. Just as in the birth of triplets, all three sons share the surname of their father; likewise in the Godhead, though devoid of birth or origin, all three persons share in the name of the Godhead, namely, God the Father, God the Son, and God the Holy Spirit. But hold it! Though each has a distinct function, they are of one union in the Godhead. In regard to this mind-challenging question, the Son of God Himself declared, "*The Father is in Me, and I in the Father [union of Godhead]*" (John 10:38).

The three persons, though each referred to as God, are somehow interconnected in information sharing, co-sovereign, co-omniscient, and co-dependent in all their decision makings and actions and are of the same essence, God. We can go on endlessly in our explanation of this phenomenal concept and yet never exhaust the Biblical teaching about an infinite God, whom Scripture revealed to be three in one but not three independent gods! Scripture has helped us identify the members of the Godhead:

> *Now when all the people were baptized, it came to pass, that Jesus also being baptized, and praying, the heaven was opened, And the Holy Ghost descended in a bodily shape like a dove upon him, and a voice came from heaven, which said, Thou art my beloved Son; in thee I am well pleased* (Luke 3:21-22, KJV).

According to Scripture, the purpose of the baptism of Jesus Christ was solely for John the Baptist to identify Jesus without a shadow of doubt as the Son of God (John 1:30-

34). And what better confirmation than the testimony of the presence of the Holy Spirit descending upon Jesus Christ and the voice of the Father coming right out of heaven saying, "*Thou [Jesus Christ] art my beloved Son; in thee I am well pleased.*"

In Matthew 28:19, Jesus Christ, after commissioning His disciples, charged, "*Go therefore and make disciples of all the nations, baptizing them in the name of the Father and the Son and the Holy Spirit.*" Here again the issue of Trinity is clearly revealed. Jesus Christ also identified the Father as a separate member when He prayed in John 11:41-42:

> *And Jesus [visible on earth] lifted up his eyes [toward Heaven], and said, Father [whose abode is in Heaven], I thank thee that thou hast heard me. And I knew that thou hearest me always: but because of the people which stand by I said it, that they may believe that thou hast sent me [from Heaven].*

The truth of the matter is that when we read the gospel of John with an open mind, we will come to the conclusion that, indeed, God has revealed Himself to us in the person of Jesus Christ. That's the central work of the apostle John, who clearly stated his purpose in the text itself, namely, to demonstrate that Jesus Christ is the Son of God: "*But these have been written that you may believe that Jesus is the Christ, the Son of God; and that believing you may have life in His name*" (John 20:31).

Now that we have a tiny bit of knowledge of who the true God is, that He manifests Himself in three distinct personalities and functions, the question is, why do many still worship creatures rather than the Creator Himself, even among Christians? We can't wait to get to chapters 4 and 5, where we shall briefly discuss the folly of idolatry and its ramifications. But before we get to those chapters, we need to take a close examination of the sovereignty of God, which is a component of the framework of this book.

2 | Overview of God's Sovereignty

*For the LORD Most High is to be feared, a great King
over all the earth. God reigns over the nations, God sits
on His holy throne* (Psalm 47:2,8).

We are about to examine another crucial component of
the essence of God, namely, sovereignty. Our grip on the
subject of sovereignty is critical to proper interpretation of
disasters in our lives. Keep in mind that it's not within the
range of this chapter to settle the issue of God's sovereignty,
a subject that has been hotly debated for centuries. We are
acutely aware that the Church for a long time has been in
division over this matter. Suffice it to say that without ample
knowledge of God's sovereignty over human affairs, no one
would dare attribute disaster to Him. On the other hand, a
measure of understanding of this subject will help us relate
to the sovereign control of God over the universe, including
disasters. There's no doubt in my mind that a grasp of this
subject will make us appreciate the saying that God is the
Lord of history!

Sovereignty is a theological word, and is a component of
God's essence as delineated previously. We noted in chapter
1 that no finite mind can fully comprehend an infinite God,

let alone define Him wholesomely. Of course, this does not in any way belittle the work of great scholars in their attempt to cast light on the God of the universe. They have done an awesome job in the field of theology in helping us comprehend who and what God is, based on God's revelation of Himself to man. We would be forever indebted to these scholars! The sublime truth remains: God is greater than our human minds can fathom—His ways are totally unfathomable! That's the truth of Scripture as in Isaiah 55:9: "*For as the heavens are higher than the earth, So are My ways higher than your ways And My thoughts than your thoughts.*" We ask, "How much higher is heaven than the earth?" The answer is in one word: immeasurable! With this in mind we define sovereignty as revealed in Scripture.

SOVEREIGNTY DEFINED

Sovereignty means that the Creator-God has absolute, supreme, airtight control of all things as He directs and superintends all events of the universe in accordance with the counsel of His will (see Ephesians 1:11).

In light of this definition, we revisit the essence of God. This, as mentioned earlier, includes sovereignty, veracity, love, eternal life, immutability, omnipresence, omniscience, omnipotence, righteousness, and justice. They are the components of His essence according to Scripture. These components stand or fall together. They are interwoven like a tapestry! We are to view them as a coherent unit. For instance, our explanation of God's sovereignty should take His justice into account. That's to say, there must be a balance between the two and in all His essence, for that matter.

With this concept in mind, we consider God's justice as a weight on one plate of the Supreme Scale of Heaven with

God's sovereignty balanced on the other. The rule of hermeneutics is that we work our way from clear passages of Scripture to the obscure ones. Scriptural references abound concerning God's justice. We shall examine just a few. Moses affirms in Deuteronomy 32:4: *"The Rock [a metaphor for God]! His work is perfect, For **all His ways are just; A God of faithfulness and without injustice, Righteous and upright** is He"* (emphasis added). In Psalm 89:14 we read that *"Righteousness and justice are the foundation of [God's] throne."* We read in Job 34:12, *"Surely, God will not act wickedly, And the Almighty will not pervert justice."* In other words, a just God cannot tilt the scale of justice in favor of anyone, no matter what. The apostle Paul, in Romans 2:11, pours concrete on this truth with these solidifying words: *"For there is no partiality with God"* (cf. Ephesians 6:9).

We concede as did the apostle Peter that some passages of Scripture are hard to understand, which unfortunately both *"the untaught and unstable distort, as they do also the rest of the Scriptures, to their own destruction"* (2 Peter 3:16). We have no excuse whatsoever for explaining the truth away just because we cannot arrive at a desired answer. Worse still, we injure ourselves when we scramble here and there and lift Scriptures out of context to defend our position even if our theology is built on sinking ground. The truth of the matter is that our failure to harmonize Scriptures will not hamper the harmony of Scriptures. Just because one has toiled day and night to solve a problem with no success, for instance in physics, does not imply that the problem is unsolvable. God is just, and on this foundational truth we commence to build the superstructure of this passage.

God is the Sovereign Creator! We ask, is it possible for any creature to have dominion over its creator? For example, can a robot, no matter how sophisticated, control its maker? We answer no to these questions! Sovereignty then as already defined means that the Creator-God has absolute, supreme, airtight control in everything as He directs and superintends all events of the universe in accordance to the counsel of His will (Ephesians 1:11). King David, in Psalm 103:19, said it aptly: *"The LORD has established His throne in the heavens, And His sovereignty rules over all."* That's right! He reigns on high; He reigns supreme (Psalm 113:5). Truly there are many things we cannot fully comprehend about God's work; nonetheless, whatever He does, comprehensible to us or not, points back to His perfect character as a righteous and just God, a subject we shall discuss in the next chapter. One may ask, "Does it mean that God is the creator of evil, too, since He is the creator of all things?"

Far from it! God is not the creator or the originator of evil. Rather, a rebellious thought was first conceived, incubated, and hatched into full-blown evil when Satan rebelled against God (Isaiah 14:12-15). That's not all; Satan was successful in deceiving a third of the angelic beings by luring them to joining him in his attempt to overthrow His creator (Revelation 12:4,7-9). Their effort failed, as we would have expected, but not without eternal repercussions. Sin was born! There and then, God made a demarcation between Him and the rebellious ones (Isaiah 14:12-16; cf. 59:1-2).

But that did not end there. After God created Adam and Eve, Satan disguised himself and deceitfully sold his lie to Eve and thus deceived Eve to do the same thing he had done in the time past, namely, to rebel against God's authority. As a result of Satan's well-crafted deception, both Adam and Eve rebelled against the rule of their heavenly Father-God (Genesis 3:1-7). Conversely, evil was born on Earth! In a

Pauline epistle we read, *"Therefore, just as through one man [Adam] sin entered into the world [by the virtue of Adam and Eve's propagation], and death through sin, and so death spread to all men, because all sinned [by virtue of our inherited sin nature]"* (Romans 5:12).

We ask, "Where was God when all these things were happening? Why didn't He in His sovereignty stop all these in the first place?" Scripture is totally silent on these questions, and so should we be. But suffice it to say, we have an illustration.

Let us assume to be members of Curiosity Joggers Club, who run twenty miles daily with our curious minds sticking out as we jog. One morning, while jogging, we passed an old Mercedes Benz parked on the street with its engine on. Two hours later on our way back, we notice that the engine is still running with no one in sight. The question then is, can we say that the owner of this Benz is a lunatic because he left his engine on all this while? No, we have no basis to make such an assertion. He may have left it on for various reasons, one of which could be to let its battery be supercharged. Here then is the real question: is the owner of the Benz under obligation to tell anyone who passes by why he left the engine of his car on? Doesn't he have the right to do what he pleases to his car? Of course he does! With that in mind, we read the words of Paul, the greatest apostle of all time:

> *What shall we say then? There is no injustice with God, is there? May it never be! For He says to Moses, "I will have mercy on whom I have mercy, and I will have compassion on whom I have compassion." So then it does not depend on the man who wills or the man who runs, but on God who has mercy. For the Scripture says to Pharaoh, "For this very purpose I raised you up, to demonstrate my power in you, and that my name*

might be proclaimed throughout the whole earth." So then He has mercy on whom He desires, and He hardens whom He desires. You will say to me then, "Why does He still find fault? For who resists His will?" On the contrary, who are you, O man, who answers back to God? The thing molded will not say to the molder, "Why did you make me like this," will it? Or does not the potter have a right over the clay, to make from the same lump one vessel for honorable use and another for common use? (Romans 9:14-21).

There are two factors that govern the passage in question. The first is the justice of God, and the second is His omniscience. The apostle knew that reading a passage like this one, *"For the Scripture says to Pharaoh, 'For this very purpose I raised you up, to demonstrate my power in you, and that my name might be proclaimed throughout the whole earth,'"* would compel one to stick a label of injustice on God. Knowing that, he thundered back at such temptation with these words: *"What shall we say then? There is no injustice with God, is there? May it never be!"*

Sadly, some, even renowned Bible communicators, though with good intention in their exposition had nonetheless misapplied this, and few other passages, which resulted in their theology of limited atonement. These, in reference to this passage, cemented their position that God in His sovereignty chose some to eternal life while rejecting others. Based on this premise they build a teaching that Jesus Christ died on the cross for the chosen ones. John Calvin, a proponent of this theology, called it a "horrible decree."[7]

---

[7] W. S. Reid, "Predestination," in *Evangelical Dictionary of Theology*, p. 937.

The truth of the matter is that if God were to have fellow judges outside of Himself, it is clear that no impartial judge would consider such ruling a just ruling. But if that's an unjust ruling, doesn't that make God an unjust God? Of course it does! Is God unjust? The apostle says, "*May it never be*!" What the apostle meant was that God, like the Mercedes Benz owner in our analogy, has the right to do what He pleases so long as His justice is not mired, or any of His essence for that matter. It's proper at this time to briefly examine the hardness of Pharaoh's heart in relation to the sovereignty of God.

HARDNESS OF PHARAOH'S HEART

What shall we say then? There is no injustice with God, is there? May it never be! For He says to Moses, "I will have mercy on whom I have mercy, and I will have compassion on whom I have compassion." So then it does not depend on the man who wills or the man who runs, but on God who has mercy. For the Scripture says to Pharaoh, "For this very purpose I raised you up, to demonstrate my power in you, and that my name might be proclaimed throughout the whole earth" (Romans 9:14-17).

No question about it! If we take Romans 9:14-17 at face value, we would be forced to conclude that Pharaoh had no choice as to the hardness of his heart, that God created him that way. In other words, God made him in such a way that he couldn't change his mind even if he had wanted to: *"For this very purpose I raised you up, to demonstrate my power in you, and that my name might be proclaimed throughout the whole earth."* We ask, if God could raise His creature for the purpose of destroying him because He is a sovereign God, what kind of God is He? The truth is that the Pauline epistle to the Romans did not give us enough information to conclude one way or the other regarding God's sovereignty. We need to go back to God's instruction to Moses in the burning bush. In the dialogue between God and Moses, God told Moses, *"But I know that [Pharaoh] the king of Egypt will not permit you to go, except under compulsion. So I will stretch out My hand and strike Egypt with all My miracles which I shall do in the midst of it; and after that he will let you go?"* (Exodus 3:19-20).

The phrase *"But I know"* is the key to the passage. It highlighted God's foreknowledge. He could have began the passage this way, "I will harden Pharaoh's heart," but He didn't. Rather, His foreknowledge reached out from eternity past to tell Moses in time the record of omniscience. "But I know that he will harden his heart because of his stubbornness." Right after God's foreknowledge, *"I know,"* was underscored, we have God's word to Moses, *"When you go back to Egypt see that you perform before Pharaoh all the wonders which I have put in your power; but I will harden his heart so that he will not let the people go"* (Exodus 4:21).

There seems to be a contradiction between Pharaoh's responsibility and God's sovereignty. But actually, there's not. A careful scrutiny of Moses' encounter with Pharaoh sheds light on this seeming contradiction. In Exodus 5:2, Pharaoh's stubbornness was magnified in his first encounter with Moses, as noted herein: *"But Pharaoh said, 'Who is the LORD that I should obey His voice to let Israel go? I do not know the LORD, and besides, I will not let Israel go.'"* Moses performed another miracle to force Pharaoh to comply, but the response was unchanged, as seen in 7:13-14: *"Yet Pharaoh's heart was hardened, and he did not listen to them, as the LORD had said. Then the LORD said to Moses, 'Pharaoh's heart is stubborn; he refuses to let the people go.'"* Let us take notice of God's comment, *"Pharaoh's heart is stubborn; he refuses to let the people go."* Did God make Pharaoh's heart stubborn? He could, but that would have jeopardized His righteous character! All along, we have been reading about the fulfillment of what God foreknew about Pharaoh's stubbornness, but that's about to be changed. God was about to apply His sovereignty to lock him up in the prison of his stubbornness (Romans 1:24). To cast light on this, the editors of New American Standard Bible said it beautifully:

> "Those who have long persisted in the ways of evil reach a point at which they are unable to distinguish right from wrong or good from evil. They grow hardened and morally incorrigible. Without doubt this was the state of Pharaoh. Being a man accustomed to the abuse of power, he steeled himself against all sense of justice and mercy. In Rom. 1:24 God is said to have given up immoral men to the path they were determined to follow. In the same way God allowed Pharaoh to follow the course he was determined to follow. God did not force him to act in any evil way nor did He by divine decree determine that Pharaoh would not repent if he so chose.[8]

God knew that he would not turn to Him and be saved. God knew that miracles would not change him to consider the God of Israel. He knew that only by pressure could he comply with God's demand to let the Israelites go (Exodus

---

[8] NASB 1995 pp. 85-86

3:19). God knew all that! That's the sweetness of omniscience! In his stubbornness, he would now serve as God's servant or a channel in two frontlines (Psalm 119:91).

First, God intended to keep Pharaoh in that state of stubbornness so that through His miraculous work He could create a frame of reference among His people Israel (Exodus 10:1-2; Psalm 78:11). Second, God wanted to use this opportunity to demonstrate His power throughout the world, as noted in Exodus 9:16-17: "*But, indeed, for this reason I have allowed you to remain [God's sovereignty kept him alive], in order to show you My power and in order to proclaim My name through all the earth. Still you exalt yourself against My people by not letting them go.*" There we have it on record! Pride, as we know, is a heinous sin, and a righteous God cannot implant a spirit of pride in anyone (James 1:13). He can only judge it wherever it rears its ugly head (Proverbs 16:5). This prepares us to examine Paul's words.

The word that the apostle Paul translated "raised you up" (Romans 9:17) in its original context in the Old Testament (Exodus 9:16) literally means "to stand."[9] Furthermore we should note in the original text that, "The form 'he' emadtika' is the Hiphil perfect of 'amad.' It would normally mean 'I caused you to stand.' But that seems to have one or two different connotations. Driver says that it means 'maintain you alive.' The causative of this verb means to continue according to him (Driver, p. 73). The LXX has the same basic sense– 'you were preserved.' But Paul bypasses the Greek and writes 'he raised you up' to show

---

[9] W. E. Vine and Merrill F. Unger, *Vine's Complete Expository Dictionary of Old and New Testament Words* (1984, 1996), p. 243.

God's absolute sovereignty over Pharaoh.'"[10] The question that seems to elude us is this: when did God raise him up? Was he born stubborn? Or programmed to be stubborn? A careful examination of how Paul used the word in Greek suggests at a point of time God freezes him so to stay in the state of his stubbornness. The truth of the matter is that God's sovereignty played no role in Pharaoh's stubbornness. He was already a stubborn king! That's what the Bible claims!

"The LORD said to Moses, 'When you go back to Egypt see that you perform before Pharaoh all the wonders which I have put in your power; but I will harden his heart so that he will not let the people go'" (Exodus 4:21). The phrase *"but I will harden his heart"* indicates the future. This clearly expels any thought that God's sovereignty controlled his heart from birth.

In essence, what God did was to allow him to remain alive and in power so that He could finish the ten plagues that were tailored to manifest His dynamic power among His people and around the world. God could have used just one plague and forced Pharaoh to comply. He could have taken Pharaoh's life after His first miraculous sign, but He didn't! He wanted to keep him alive so as to accomplish His plan and purpose. God reserved the tenth plague as His last straw to force Pharaoh to comply: *"But I know that [Pharaoh] the king of Egypt will not permit you to go, except under compulsion. So I will stretch out My hand and strike Egypt with all My miracles* [ten of them] *which I shall do in*

---

[10] Brown, Francis, S. R. Driver and Charles A. Briggs. *The New Brown-Driver-Briggs-Gesenius Hebrew and English Lexicon* (Peabody, MA: Hendrickson, 1979), p. 162.

the midst of it; and after that [the tenth one] *he will let you go*" (Exodus 3:19-20). With this insight we can read this Pauline epistle afresh:

> *What shall we say then? There is no injustice with God, is there? May it never be! For He says to Moses, "I will have mercy on whom I have mercy, and I will have compassion on whom I have compassion." So then it does not depend on the man who wills or the man who runs, but on God who has mercy. For the Scripture says to Pharaoh, "**For this very purpose I raised you up** ['I have allowed you to remain,' (Exodus 9:16)], **to demonstrate my power in you, and that my name might be proclaimed throughout the whole earth**"* (Romans 9:14-17, emphasis added).

Furthermore, God in His infinite wisdom and sovereignty made the decision to demonstrate His power when that particular pharaoh was on the throne. We noted that a handful of pharaohs who were not friendly to the Israelites had come and gone, but God waited. He could have even waited until another pharaoh came to the throne and still have been within the 400 years that He foretold to Abraham (Genesis 15:13), but He didn't. He emptied His wrath on this pharaoh for reasons known to the Creator-God alone!

"I will have mercy on whom I have mercy, and I will have compassion on whom I have compassion." This particular stubborn pharaoh was the object of God's wrath while others were spared. Why?

> *On the contrary, who are you, O man, who answers back to God? The thing molded will not say to the*

molder, "Why did you make me like this," will it? Or
does not the potter have a right over the clay, to make
from the same lump one vessel for honorable use and
another for common use? (Romans 9:20-21).

God decides the time, the place, and the means of accomplishing His will and purpose. We have no say in His decision-making!

In a nutshell, God in His sovereign, infinite wisdom created both angelic and human beings as free agents with volitional responsibilities, while He is ever ready to hold all accountable for their decisions and actions. Sovereignty then superintends every decision and every action to ensure that it does not interfere with divine decrees, as Dr. Paul Enns stated:

> The decrees are reflected in Ephesians 1:11 in that He "works all things after the counsel of His will." Question 7 of the Westminster Shorter Confession states: "The decrees of God are his eternal purpose, according to the counsel of his will, whereby, for his own glory, he hath ordained whatsoever comes to pass."[11]

I believe that the free will of man is one aspect of that which "he hath ordained."

THE FREE WILL OF MAN

Primarily, two schools of thought exist with regard to the will of man in relation to God's sovereignty. One idea is that man has free will and the other is that man is not a free agent.

---

[11] Paul Enns, *The Moody Handbook of Theology* (Moody Press: Chicago, 1989), p. 204.

Our attempt is not to settle once and for all the tension between these two camps. Nevertheless, Scriptures abound in favor of the position that God in His sovereignty created man with the freedom to choose. In Genesis 1:26, we read, "*Then God said, 'Let Us make man in Our image, according to Our likeness; and let them rule over the fish of the sea and over the birds of the sky and over the cattle and over all the earth, and over every creeping thing that creeps on the earth.'*"

In essence, when God said, "*Let Us make man in Our image, according to Our likeness,*" He was saying, "Let us create man as an intellectual being, with self-consciousness and self-determination." This is the substance of God's image! God has a will, and so He chooses to bestow this aspect of His image on man. That's God's prerogative! That's divine design!

That's not all. God delegated to Adam the authority to name all the animals at will, as seen in Genesis 2:19-20:

> *And out of the ground the LORD God formed every beast of the field and every bird of the sky, and brought them to the man to see what he would call them; and whatever the man called a living creature, that was its name. And the man gave names to all the cattle, and to the birds of the sky, and to every beast of the field.*

In addition to giving Adam the privilege of naming all the animals, God equally put Adam in a classroom, so to say, in order to test his ability to exercise his free will. Herein is the one and only test in the garden:

> *Then the LORD God took the man and put him into the garden of Eden to cultivate it and keep it. And the LORD God commanded the man, saying, "From any tree of the garden you may eat freely; but from the tree*

of the knowledge of good and evil you shall not eat, for in the day that you [exercise your free will and] eat from it you will surely die" (Genesis 2:15-17).

That's a test of the will! Let there be no misunderstanding. The fact that man is created in the image of God does not in any way put man on par with God in His sovereignty; nor does it imply that man is free to do all he wishes, whenever and wherever. Rather, in the eternal counsel of God, He made a decision to create man as a free agent with limited boundaries. I used the word *limited* because though man has free will, there are things that he cannot do even if he wants to, and there are things God will compel and impel man to do even if he has a negative volition. This is because, on the one hand, man is created as a free agent; on the other, man is equally a slave of his Creator-God (Psalm 119:91). This is like raising cattle in a fenced ranch where there's limited freedom for them to wander here and there within the ranch. They cannot go beyond the set boundaries even if they want to. That's how God created us—with limitations! For instance, man is incapable of destroying the planet, even if he wants to do so.

In the case of Adam and Eve, both used their free will against God's prohibition, and the consequence was not only their spiritual death but that of the entire world (Romans 5:12). Some have argued that after the fall man's will was diseased, so to say; as a result, man can no longer make any decision apart from God working in man. This is where the bridge between the two schools of thoughts actually collapsed.

When one carefully scrutinizes the Scriptures, it becomes clear that man is still a responsible agent, as Adam was before the fall. Since the subject of sovereignty is not our main focus, we shall examine just four passages, two in the Old Testament and two in the New.

In the Old Testament, Moses wrote,

> *Now when Pharaoh had let the people go, God did not lead them by the way of the land of the Philistines, even though it was near; for God said, "The people might change their minds when they see war, and return to Egypt [free will underscored]." Hence God led the people around by the way of the wilderness to the Red Sea; and the sons of Israel went up in martial array from the land of Egypt* (Exodus 13:17-18).

It's clear that if God, in His omniscience, had not taken them by the way of the wilderness, they could have gone against God's plan, which is to bring them to the Promised Land. They could have exercised their free will and made their way back to Egypt. That's exactly what God said: *"The people might change their minds when they see war, and return to Egypt."*

The second passage is in the book of Isaiah. The prophet Isaiah, through the Holy Spirit, ushered an invitation to the unbelieving Jews, and to anyone today for that matter, saying, *"Ho! Every one who thirsts, come to the waters; And you who have no money come, buy and eat. Come, buy wine and milk Without money and without cost"* (Isaiah 55:1).

It's obvious that's Isaiah's invitation was based on the fact that those whom this message was addressed to were capable of responding to his call. While they were not capable of understanding Isaiah's message apart from the illuminating ministry of God the Holy Spirit, nonetheless they were capable of making a choice to give the prophet a hearing. That's where man's free will comes into focus.

We see the same scenario in the New Testament. The Lord, speaking to the crowd, gave an invitation to the unsaved, saying, "*Come to Me, all who are weary and heavy-laden, and I will give you rest. Take My yoke upon you and learn from Me, for I am gentle and humble in heart, and you will find rest for your souls. For My yoke is easy and My burden is light*" (Matthew 11:28-30).

Obviously the invitation is made to all, not just to a few, but to all who are thirsty. This invitation, like Isaiah's, is based on the fact that man has the ability to give the message a hearing. We know that unsaved man cannot comprehend spiritual things (1 Corinthians 2:14), but he has the ability to choose to go and give the messenger a hearing. That's free will! We see this all the time. Many times people out of their own volition attend gospel festivals and still come back unsaved. The fact that they did go underlines one's freedom to choose. Saul of Tarsus before he was saved was a perfect example. He was present when Stephen gave the most systematic gospel message (Acts 7), which Saul rejected. He used his free will to kick against the goads, as our Lord indicated (Acts 26:14).

We pick up another story in Acts 10:1-2: "*Now there was a man at Caesarea named Cornelius, a centurion of what was called the Italian cohort, a devout man and one who feared God with all his household, and gave many alms to the Jewish people and prayed to God continually.*"

Here was a Gentile believer. At one point in his life he became aware that there must be a supreme being out there and desired a relationship with this being. In his unquenchable thirst, he made the choice, though spiritually dead, to seek out the God of the Jews, as we see from the quoted passage. That's free will in operation!

69

We could go on and on citing Scriptures, but that will result in a detour from our main subject. If we choose to go against the principles of divine establishment, sooner or later God will respond in kind. That's exactly what the Bible teaches! This prepares us to examine, in the next chapter, the integrity of God, which will further cast a beam of light on God's righteousness and justice as they relate to disasters.

3 | The Integrity of God

"Righteousness and justice are the foundation of Your throne [integrity]" (Psalm 89:14). This is one of the finest passages of Scripture, which I believe shall throw much needed light on the bedrock of God's integrity.

Civil engineers will agree that the strength of any building is measured by the strength of its foundation. This implies that any crack in a foundation is a crack in its structure at large. Likewise, the integrity of God is built on the foundation of His righteousness and justice, and so any compromise of His righteousness or justice is a compromise of His integrity as a whole. This truth is fundamental to the foundation of this book.

Often we find ourselves guilty of humanizing God. We assign God human attributes and behavioral patterns and consequently explain God's way of doing things from the human point of view. Obviously that's a colossal error on our part! We do this in many ways. For instance, we assign human love, which is nothing but a balloon of emotion, to God and then explain the love of God as we would explain human love. We assign human emotion to God and then stick a sentimental label on Him. On the contrary, God is neither human (Hosea 11:9) nor sentimental (Numbers 23:19)! The truth of the matter is that there is an immeasurable gap between us and God: "'*For My thoughts are not your thoughts, Nor are your ways My ways,' declares the LORD. 'For as the heavens are higher than the earth, So are My ways higher than your ways And My thoughts than your thoughts'*" (Isaiah 55:8-9). Now we are poised to examine briefly the dual components of the integrity of God, namely, righteousness and justice. Let us begin with righteousness.

RIGHTEOUSNESS

In brief, righteousness is a state of absolute holiness, moral and majestic purity, totally devoid of evil or sin. "Because God is morally pure, He cannot condone evil or have any relationship to it (Psalm 11:4-6). In His holiness, God is the moral and ethical standard; He is the law. He sets the standard."[12] In comparison, man possesses relative righteousness, but God is absolute righteousness. It's a component of His essence! In His righteous standard, God demands that His creatures be holy just as He is holy (Leviticus 19:2). We cannot get around His injunction. God has spoken! But again, we know that none of us is capable of being holy unless He makes us holy. Of course, God makes us holy through the imputation of His righteousness when we trust in His Son Jesus Christ alone for our salvation (Genesis 15:6; cf. Romans 3:22; 2 Corinthians 5:21; Hebrews 10:10).[13]

God must do everything to preserve His righteousness. In other words, He cannot look the other way when His laws

[12] Ibid., p.193.

[13] Moses C. Onwubiko, *Riding the Death Train.*

or laws of divine establishment are violated. This is true of any government with integrity. It cannot look the other way when its citizens violate laws that govern its subjects. Likewise, God's righteousness stands on guard to condemn anyone who shows no regard for His injunctions. This clears the table for us to examine the other half of His integrity, namely, justice.

THE JUSTICE OF GOD

Nature proves that we are people of sentiment. No question about it! The costly mistake on our part is to think that God is equally sentimental. God is a judge. The sublime truth is that sentiment cannot co-exist with justice; sentimentalism in a court of law is a recipe for partiality. On the other hand, Scripture settles it once and for all that with God there's no partiality (Romans 2:11; cf. Job 34:12). He is a God of justice (Ezra 9:15)! Contrary to public opinion, God's point of contact with us after the fall is not love. It is justice. He meets with us at the hill of Golgotha where His justice crushed His Son Jesus Christ mercilessly on the cross of Calvary (Isaiah 53:3-10). That is to say, without the cross, there can be no reconciliation or peace between sinful man and a just God!

So, justice is the point of contact between a Holy God and sinful man. His justice reigns supreme in all He does for and through us! This does not in any way eliminate the love of God. God is love. We know that (1 John 4:8). His love for us is undiminished no matter our status quo (Jeremiah 31:3). After all, it's out of His unfailing love that He offered His uniquely born Son, the Lord Jesus Christ, as a substitute, in payment for our sins (John 3:16; cf. Romans 5:8). His love, nonetheless, is not a point of contact with us. Suffice it to say,

God's love is entirely different from human love.

Human love is nothing but a balloon of emotion, as we previously stated. It waxes and wanes and feeds sentiments like wildfire. That's totally the opposite of God's love, which is good news for us all. This is because none of us in our sinful nature has what it takes to attract God's love. To say this in a simple way, we make God mad all the time, because in us dwells nothing good (Romans 7:14-25; Ecclesiastes 7:20). That's true even for the best of the best! The Psalmist recognized this and asked, "*If thou, LORD, shouldest mark iniquities, O Lord, who shall stand?*" (Psalm 130:3, KJV). The answer is obvious! God deals with us on the basis of His matchless grace. Jeremiah, recalling God's grace, said, "*This I recall to my mind, Therefore I have hope. The LORD'S lovingkindnesses indeed never cease, For His compassions never fail. They are new every morning; Great is Your faithfulness*" (Lamentations 3:21-23).

Keeping things in perceptive, the justice of God and His righteousness go in tandem. They compliment one another for the preservation of God's integrity. In other words, when there is even one iota of a violation of His righteous standard, His righteousness will condemn the action, and consequently His justice will respond swiftly to satisfy righteousness. This is the crossroads where liberal theologians seem to have lost their compass. This is the junction where they have gotten lost when it comes to ascribing disasters to God. They conclude, "A sweet, caring, loving God can never, ever do anything harmful to anyone." They reach a conclusion that 9/11 could never be the handiwork of God. These forget that the begotten Son of God, whom the Father loves dearly, was bitterly crushed on the cross by God Himself. My friend, when we think of it, that's justice superseding love! God's justice always reigns supreme! Isaiah prophesies,

> *Surely our griefs He Himself bore, And our sorrows He carried; Yet we ourselves esteemed Him stricken,* **Smitten of God***, and afflicted. But He was pierced through for our transgressions, He was crushed for our iniquities; The chastening for our well-being fell upon Him, And by His scourging we are healed...***But the LORD was pleased To crush Him, putting Him to grief***"* (Isaiah 53:4-10, emphasis added).

You read the last sentence correctly! *"But the LORD was pleased To crush Him, putting Him to grief."* Why? He had to do so in order to satisfy His righteousness. Sin was committed; His righteousness condemned it out right. That set the stage for the justice of God to weigh in; sin must be judged! A penalty must be paid! So God in His infinite grace sent His Son as a substitute. His justice followed through by rendering judgment on His Son! You see, the issue is justice, not love. That explains why God could destroy Noah's world with a flood and rain fire and brimstone on Sodom and Gomorrah. That's justice! We shall examine all this in detail as our work progresses.

Someone may ask, "Why are many evil people roaming around successfully with no consequences in sight?" You are not alone in asking such a question. In Jeremiah's account we read, *"Righteous are You, O LORD, that I would plead my case with You; Indeed I would discuss matters of justice with You: Why has the way of the wicked prospered? Why are all those who deal in treachery at ease?"* (Jeremiah 12:1).

That's a good question. But do you know that were not for the grace of God, none of us would still be alive today

(Psalm 130:3)? The sublime truth is that justice delayed is not justice denied. Just because someone has been dubious in all his business activities and getting away with it does not in any way mean that God is unconcerned. Just because someone has been violating every norm and standard with no consequences does not in any way nullify the justice of God. But by delaying justice, God is showing us another aspect of His awesome character. He is showing us that He is a compassionate God, a God of long-suffering! This is revealed in Scripture, for example in Exodus 34:6-7:

> *Then the LORD passed by in front of him and proclaimed, "The LORD, the LORD God, compassionate and gracious, slow to anger, and abounding in lovingkindness and truth; who keeps lovingkindness for thousands, who forgives iniquity, transgression and sin; yet He will by no means leave the guilty unpunished."*

That's right! "*He will by no means leave the guilty unpunished.*" God gives us ample time to mend our ways. That's His grace in action! But there is a limit to which He can tolerate us before He administers justice. That's true of Judah, as we shall explore in detail when we get to chapter 9. But let's underscore God's long-suffering by reading the words of prophet Jeremiah to Judah:

> "*The LORD, the God of their fathers, **sent word to them again and again** by His messengers, because He had compassion on His people and on His dwelling place; but they continually mocked the messengers of God, despised His words and scoffed at His prophets, until the wrath of the LORD arose against His people, until there was no remedy. **Therefore He brought up against them the king of the Chaldeans who slew their***

*young men with the sword in the house of their sanc-
tuary, and had no compassion on young man or virgin,
old man or infirm; He gave them all into his hand*" (2
Chronicles 36:15-17, emphasis added).

Therein is the manifestation of the justice of God! The
cup of God's longsuffering was filled to the brim so that His
only recourse was to render judgment on Judah. That's justice! The justice of God always prevails!

This sums up part 1 of our study; we hope you have been
edified so far. This clears the way for us to begin an in-depth
examination of how God communicates to us by means of
disasters.

PART II | Why Do People Experience Disaster, One After Another?

Part II is dedicated to answering the question as to why everyone goes through disasters in life. Why do both carnal and spiritual believers suffer the same fate in disaster? Idolatry attracts maximum divine discipline from the Supreme Court of Heaven!

4 | The Folly of Idolatry

Then God spoke all these words, saying, "I am the LORD your God, who brought you out of the land of Egypt, out of the house of slavery. You shall have no other gods before Me. You shall not make for yourself an idol, or any likeness of what is in heaven above or on the earth beneath or in the water under the earth. You shall not worship them or serve them; for I, the LORD your God, am a jealous God, visiting the iniquity of the fathers on the children, on the third and the fourth generations of those who hate Me" (Exodus 20:1-5).

Generally, people tend to be ignorant of the fact that idolatry is not just a creature worshipping a creature; it is having communion with demons! We shall develop this concept later. Tragically, any nation that is involves in idolatry sets itself up for national disasters, which God in His justice administers from the Supreme Court of Heaven. That goes for individuals, too! God strongly opposed idolatry and consequently punishes anyone who takes part in any form of idol worship. What's even more frightening is that some believers are involved in what I call whitewashed idolatry, a subject we shall uncover in the next chapter. God opposes idolatry in every sense of the word! This we know from His commandment to the Jews through Moses: "*You shall not make for yourself an idol, or any likeness of what is in heaven above or on the earth beneath or in the water under the earth. You shall not worship them or serve them.*" That's God's Word!

At this crossroad we ask, "What is idolatry?"

> Ultimately in the [New Testament] idolatry came to mean, not only to giving to any creature or human creation the honor or devotion which belonged to God alone, but the giving of any human desire a precedence over God's will [1 Corinthians 10:14; Galatians 5:20; Colossians 3:5; 1 Peter 4:3].[14]

It is a creature honoring and worshipping creation in all its forms and shapes.

It is comforting that the true God of the universe has never left Himself without evidence that He exists, as previously delineated in chapter 1. God's revelation of Himself to man through natural manifestation of His glorious power is clearly visible, as the apostle Paul cited in Romans 1:20: "*For since the creation of the world His invisible attributes, His eternal power and divine nature, have been clearly seen, being understood through what has been made, so that they are without excuse.*" It's in God's nature to make Himself known to His creatures! Think of it this way: an anxious pen pal is flying from China to the United States of America to meet a long-time friend he has only known through writings; wouldn't he give his anxious friend in the U.S. a clue about how to identify him when he arrives at the airport? Of course

---

[14] James Orr, ed., *The International Standard Bible Encyclopaedia* (Grand Rapids: Eerdmans, 1930), p. 1448.

he would. Then we ask, "Would the Creator-God, whose intention in creation of man in the first place is to have a relationship with man and for man to glorify Him, not give man all the clues man would need to know that a supreme, intelligent being must have created man?"

The sublime truth is that God in His infinite wisdom revealed Himself to us in such away that we have no excuse to not have a personal relationship with Him if we so desire. Every human being who inhabits our planet Earth knows within himself that there is a supreme, intelligent Being who some way, somehow, in a miraculous way, brought everything into existence. However when it comes to accepting the truth in our minds concerning this supreme Being, three groups of people emerged.

The first group is what I called "suppressionists." This group knows that a supreme Being exists but chooses to suppress the truth of His existence within them. They diverge into evolutionism, atheism, and the like. They would be quick to accept Charles Darwin's theory of evolution or his disciples' big bang theory, rather than accept a biblical argument such as the teleological argument. This argument deduces that "order and useful arrangement in a system imply [not chance but] intelligence and purpose in the organizing cause."[15]

Dr. Paul Enns elaborated on this theory:

The world everywhere evidences intelligence, purpose and harmony; [suggesting] a master architect behind all this evidence. The psalmist sees the mag-

---

[15] Henry C. Thiessen, *Lectures in Systematic Theology* (Grand Rapids: Eerdmans, 1977), p. 28.

nificent of God's creation in the universe and recognizes that it testifies to His existence (Psalm 8:3-4; 19:1-4). God's harmony is observed throughout the universe and world: the sun being ninety-three million miles distant is precisely right for an adequate climate on earth; the moon's distance of two hundred and forty thousand miles provides tides at proper level; the earth's tilts provides the season. A conclusion is clear that God, the Master Designer, has created this magnificent universe. He added that the alternative, that the world happened "by chance," is no more possible than a monkey's being able to create a work of Shakespeare on a typewriter by haphazard play on the keys.[16]

The second group is what I referred to as "misguided." This group of people, by observing the manifestations of God's firmament in creation, come to the conclusion that there must be a supreme Being out there somewhere, and they desire a relationship with this Being. Through misinformation stemming from ancestry and cultural influences, they seek to establish contact with this being through idolatry. This explains why almost every country is involved in one form of idol worship or another. We mentioned earlier a nation with 33 million gods and goddesses. That number is not an exaggeration. People of that culture worship almost everything, ranging from human beings, cows, rabbits, and rats to inanimate things such as stones, bones, mountains, and the like. They remain in ignorance until the Mind Reader, the true God who knows the heart of men, sends

---

[16] Enns, *The Moody Handbook of Theology*, pp. 183-241.

them light-bearers to lead them to the True God. We see the reality of this 2,000 years ago, when the apostle Paul went to idol worshipers in Acts 17:16-34. We have witnessed in our missionary campaigns thousands of these people in bondage to idolatry embracing the true and only God of the universe by grace through faith—plus nothing, minus nothing—in Christ alone. What a freedom!

This brings us to the third group of people, which I referred to as the "true seekers." They too have come to the conclusion that there must be a supreme Being out there; however, they reject outright the idea of Him being found in objects of creation. Consequently, they desire to know Him apart from idolatry. Invariably, God has done everything within His power to make Himself known to such yearning hearts. For instance, in the past, He revealed Himself to man through His angelic creatures, dreams, and visions or by speaking directly to individuals, as He did with Abraham (Genesis 12:1-3), Moses (Exodus 3), and others. It is remarkable how one is taken aback when one hears intriguing testimonies about how true seekers yearned for the true God and consequently found Him. One wonders, "What sense do creatures make out of worshipping creatures?"

A provocative illustration can be used to challenge those who are entangled in idolatry, an illustration tailored to stimulate the thinking of those who worship things in the heavens above like the sun, the moon, and the stars; creatures of the air, like birds; creations on the land, such as human beings, animals, trees, and stones; and creatures of the waters, such as fish and water snakes. We ask ourselves, who is superior, that which is created or the one who created it? Consider the golden image that Nebuchadnezzar made several millennia ago according to Scripture (Daniel 3:1). We pose the question, "Who can we credit with power, lordship, and honor, the image or the goldsmith?" Do we hear *gold-smith*? That's right! The goldsmith had all the power within himself to fashion the image in any desirable shape. Then it does not make sense that glory, praise, and worship be directed to the image itself and not to the goldsmith for his superb handiwork.

But hold it! That's exactly what we do when we create things and make them objects of worship. That's folly! Psalm 96:7 commands us, "*Ascribe to the LORD, O families of the peoples, Ascribe to the LORD glory and strength.*" My friends, images have no life, no power, and cannot be of help in times of need! It boils down to this: we become fools when we worship the handiwork of man or God rather than the Creator-God Himself, who created everything therein. To this end, the Psalmist wrote,

> *For all the gods of the peoples are idols, But the LORD made the heavens. Splendor and majesty are before Him, Strength and beauty are in His sanctuary* (Psalm 96:5-6).

> *But our God is in the heavens; He does whatever He pleases. Their idols are silver and gold, The work of man's hands. They have mouths, but they cannot speak; They have eyes, but they cannot see; They have ears, but they cannot hear; They have noses, but they cannot smell; They have hands, but they cannot feel; They have feet, but they cannot walk; They cannot make a sound with their throat. Those who make them will become like them, Everyone who trusts in them [will be like them]* (Psalm 115:3-8).

That's not all! The folly of idolatry is further expounded in Jeremiah 10:3-5:

> *For the customs of the peoples are delusion; Because it is wood cut from the forest, The work of the hands of a craftsman with a cutting tool. They decorate it with silver and with gold; They fasten it with nails and with hammers So that it will not totter. Like a scarecrow in a cucumber field are they, And they cannot speak; They must be carried, Because they cannot walk! Do not fear them, For they can do no harm, Nor can they do any good.*

Read it a second time! "*They fasten it with nails and with hammers So that it will not totter,*" and "*They must be carried, Because they cannot walk!*"

My friend, let us be sober in our thinking! How can something that requires our help to make it stand be capable of helping us stand on our feet physically, materially, financially, and otherwise? Or how can idols that have ears but cannot hear be able to hear our cry when we call for help in times of need? They cannot!

The words of the true God spoken through the prophet Jeremiah are striking: "*Thus you shall say to them [idolaters], 'The gods that did not make the heavens and the earth will perish from the earth and from under the heavens'*" (Jeremiah 10:11). The annals of history are piled high with the fulfillment of Jeremiah's prophesy! Where did many of those idols in the Asian peninsula go when the tsunami struck years ago? They were washed away! They couldn't escape as some people did because they could not walk nor run. They could not help themselves escape a historic disaster, let alone help anyone else. What happened to many of those voodoos of

New Orleans in the midst of Hurricane Katrina? Washed away too? Couldn't help anyone? Why then do we worship and ascribe glory to idols? Folly, is it not?

"*Thus says the Lord GOD, 'I will also destroy the idols And make the images cease*'" (Ezekiel 30:13). Furthermore, "*The gods [idols] that did not make the heavens and the earth will perish from the earth and from under the heavens*" (Jeremiah 10:11). God has spoken; that settles it! If God says, "They will perish," He will make good on His Word! The question then is, why do we worship those things that are destined to perish? Why do we worship things that, in times of need or disaster, cannot provide or defend themselves, let alone anyone else? But as for the true God, Jeremiah says again,

There is none like You, O LORD; You are great, and great is Your name in might. Who would not fear You, O King of the nations? Indeed it is Your due! For among all the wise men of the nations And in all their kingdoms, There is none like You. But they are altogether stupid and foolish In their discipline of delusion—their idol is wood! Beaten silver is brought from Tarshish, And gold from Uphaz, The work of a craftsman and of the hands of a goldsmith; Violet and purple are their clothing; blue and purple is their clothing: They are all the work of skilled men. But the LORD is the true God; He is the living God and the everlasting King. At His wrath the earth quakes, And the nations cannot endure His indignation…It is He who made the earth by His power, Who established the world by His wisdom; And by His understanding He has stretched out the heavens…Every man is stupid, devoid of knowledge; Every goldsmith is put to shame by his idols; For his molten images are deceitful, And there is no breath in them. They are worthless, a work of mockery; In the time of their punishment they will perish (Jeremiah 10:6-15; cf. Psalm 135:15-18).

This brings us to the danger zone of idolatry.

MAN'S WORSHIP OF DEMONS

Idolatry is one of the major reasons why a righteous and just God disciplines individuals or a nation as a whole. We ask, "Since idols are without life, why then does God often punish a city or nation severely because of its involvement in idolatry?" The answer is not too hard to come by! Idolatry is one of the fewer avenues of direct contact with demons; consequently, our worship of idols is tantamount to a communion with demons! Through this medium, demons influence us to influence the world around us. We do so through propagation of the doctrines of demons, which in turn causes evil to skyrocket. When the cup of evil is full to the brim in a nation, God chooses the time and the manner to rain down disaster so as to curtail evil in that part of the world. Evil must be checked! That's the justice of God. The ignorance of what we do when we offer sacrifices to idols is explained in a Pauline epistle:

> *Look at the nation Israel; are not those who eat the sacrifices sharers in the altar? What do I mean then? That a thing sacrificed to idols is anything, or that an idol is anything? No, but I say that the things which the Gentiles sacrifice, they sacrifice to demons and not to God; and I do not want you to become sharers in demons* (1 Corinthians 10:18-20).

The apostle John wrote, "*And the rest of mankind, who were not killed by these plagues [of the Great Tribulation], did not repent of the works of their hands, so as not to worship demons [by means of]...the idols of gold and of silver and of brass and of stone and of wood, which can neither see nor hear nor walk*" (Revelation 9:20).

The sublime truth is that God was dead serious when He spoke to Moses in Exodus 22:20 signifying that He does not, cannot, and will not tolerate idolatry: "*He who sacrifices to any god, other than to the LORD alone, shall be utterly destroyed.*"

Simply stated, when idolatry reigns supreme in a nation, the fire of evil escalates and consequently engulfs every facet of society. A nation that finds itself in this state is actually begging for a disaster, as Ezekiel 7:5 foretold: "*Thus says the Lord GOD, 'A disaster, unique disaster, behold it is coming!*'" God must extinguish the flame of evil. Looking back, we can say that Hurricane Katrina, the tsunami of 2004, and the United States' 9/11 were unique disasters!

Again we ask, "When a disaster occurs in someone's life or in a nation, who is responsible?" Do we hear, "Satan and his minions"? Wrong! The Lord claims responsibility, as we noted in the book of Isaiah 45:7: "*[I Am] the One forming light and creating darkness, Causing well-being and creating calamity; I am the LORD who does all these.*" "I create calamities; I manufacture them!" Why would He not? Think of it, as parents with children in our homes, what do we do when our house is in total chaos because of our children's delinquency? Do we not devise appropriate measures to bring our house into order? Do we not think in a hurry what we should do to curtail and deter delinquent behaviors? Of course we do! Why then do we blame God if He employs a disastrous means to keep His world from self-destruction? Why do we say, "How can a loving God do such and such a thing?" when we can as parents? But there is another subtle form of idolatry, the worst kind, which often entraps many believers in the Lord Jesus Christ. This is the subject of the next chapter.

5 | Whitewashed Idolatry

Therefore consider the members of your earthly body as dead to immorality, impurity, passion, evil desire, and greed, which amounts to idolatry (Colossians 3:5).

Little children, guard yourselves from idols (1 John 5:21).

Two thousand years ago, Jesus Christ sharply rebuked the religious crowd of His day with these striking words:

"You blind Pharisee, first clean the inside of the cup and of the dish, so that the outside of it may become clean also. Woe to you, scribes and Pharisees, hypocrites! For you are like whitewashed tombs which on the outside appear beautiful, but inside they are full of dead men's bones and all uncleanness" (Matthew 23:26-27).

He also said, *"Woe to you! For you are like concealed tombs, and the people who walk over them are unaware of it"* (Luke 11:44).

Whitewashed and *concealed tomb*—those words say it all! Too often when we hear the word *idolatry*, our minds quickly take off to Africa and Asia, where idol temples can be sighted on street corners. It never dawns on us that we may actually have concealed idols in our own homes, backyards, banks—even in our hearts! Of course it's easier to see a conventional idol in an obscure temple and look the other way in a hurry than it is to spot a potential site for a gold mine on our farmland and not be mesmerized. What the obscure image may be to the ignorant the preoccupation with the gold site may be to the well informed. Both could find themselves involved in idolatry!

Recall that *idolatry* means "not only to giving to any creature or human creation the honor or devotion which belonged to God alone, but the giving of any human desire a precedence over God's will."[17] Simply put, concealed idolatry is the worst kind, because of its deceptive nature! In view of this, we shall discuss in this chapter three types of concealed idolatries, namely, idolatry in the heart, idolatry of money, and idolatry of materialism.

IDOLATRY IN THE HEART

> *Son of man, these men have set up their idols in their hearts and have put right before their faces the stumbling block of their iniquity Should I be consulted by them [through prayer] at all?* (Ezekiel 14:3).

King Solomon, the wisest man who ever lived, exhorts us in Proverbs 4:23 to "*Watch over [our] heart[s] with all diligence, For from [them] flow the springs of life.*" But we tend to forget that our hearts are battlefields. They are information-processing and decision-making centers. It goes

_____

[17] Orr, *The International Standard Bible Encyclopaedia*, p. 1448.

without saying that what goes into our hearts comes out in our actions—in other words *garbage in, garbage out*. We have heard it said many times that what is outside cannot ruin a person; it is what is inside. Jesus Christ Himself stated this phenomenal truth, as recorded in the book of Mark:

> *And He said to them, "Are you so lacking in under-standing also? Do you not understand that whatever goes into the man from outside cannot defile him"...And He was saying, "That which proceeds out of the man, that is what defiles the man. For from within, out of the heart of men, proceed the evil thoughts, fornications, thefts, murders, adulteries, deeds of coveting and wickedness, as well as deceit, sen-suality, envy, slander, pride and foolishness. All these evil things proceed from within and defile the man"* (Mark 7:18-23).

Therein we have it: from within, out of the heart of men, evil thoughts are conceived, incubated and hatched into action. That explains why God judges us on the basis of the contents of our hearts (1 Samuel 16:7). Our hearts are where every action in life is manufactured. The decision to obey or not obey God's mandates and love Him with all our might is made in our hearts. But the question arises, how can we have idols in our hearts?

The answer is not all that simple. We have said previously that concealed idolatry is the worst kind because of its decep-tive nature. It is idolatry that goes on in our hearts. It's so concealed that we may actually be involved in demon wor-ship through idolatry, as we noted before, and not even realize it. Its subtlety is not noticeable apart from the guiding light of the Word of God. What's even more frightening and deceiving is that we can be very active in our local church and still be trapped in the deceptive chamber of idolatry.

This type of idolatry often spins off into different directions. For example, we may have people whom we idolize in our hearts, with their pictures all over our houses, in our wallets, purses, and wherever. That's tantamount to carrying idols in our hearts. What's more, if there is a contest between attending a church service or going to see those people if they are in town, going to see them wins the contest handily. That's idolatry of the heart in light of our definition, giving to any creature or human creation the honor or devotion that belongs to God alone. We say, what's the big deal if we are just going to see our icons for a day? It *is* a big deal! At that point, we are saying in our hearts that our fellowship with our visiting idols is more important than our fellowship with God. That's equivalent to idolatry! In fact, the apostle Paul taught that our attitude toward things can be translated into idolatry: "*Therefore consider the members of your earthly body as dead to immorality, impurity, passion, evil desire, and greed, which amounts to idolatry*" (Colossians 3:5). In essence, idolatry is not just worshipping carved images; it's equally giving the first place in our hearts to anything over God's will! He concluded that such behavior does and will incur the wrath of God (Colossians 3:6). This prepares us to examine another type of concealed idolatry.

IDOLATRY OF MONEY

> *No man can serve two masters: for either he will hate the one, and love the other; or else he will hold to the one, and despise the other. Ye cannot serve God and mammon [money]* (Matthew 6:24, KJV).

God and money are portrayed not as employers, but as slave owners. A man may work for two employers, but since "single ownership and full time service are the essence of slavery" (Tasker)[18], he cannot serve two slave owners. Either God is served with single-eyed devotion or He is not served at all. Attempts to divide loyalty betray not partial commitment to discipleship but deep-seated commitment to idolatry.[19]

Money in itself is a good thing if pursued and used in a right way. Often we misquote Scripture by saying that money is the root of all evil; on the contrary, 1 Timothy 6:10 states, "*For the love of money is a root of all sorts of evil, and some by longing for it have wandered away from the faith [doctrinal truth], and pierced themselves with many griefs.*" It's our love of money that makes the difference! It's "*love of money*" that is the taproot of "*all sorts of evil.*" No question about it, our attitude toward money will make or break us in life.

Many of our jails are filled to maximum capacity by people who have "*pierced themselves with many griefs*" because of their love for money. Many marriages and friendships have been wrecked because of attitudes toward money.

One may ask, "How can our pursuit of it be synonymous to idolatry?" The answer is buried in one's attitude. We reiterate our New Testament meaning of idolatry: not only the giving to any creature or human creation the honor or devotion that belongs to God alone, but also giving precedence to any human desire over God's will. The truth again is that

---

18 Tasker, R. V. G. *The Gospel According to St. Matthew: An Introduction and Commentary.* London: IVP, 1961

19 Frank E. Gaebelein, *The Expositor's Bible Commentary* (Zondervan, 1984), 8:178-179.

"No man can serve two masters: for either he will hate the one, and love the other; or else he will hold to the one, and despise the other. Ye cannot serve God and mammon [money]" (Matthew 6:24, KJV). Jesus Christ was emphatic in His assertion! We cannot serve or be preoccupied with God and at the same time be preoccupied with money. One or the other will have to be shortchanged! God or money—which one will come first? That is the issue! That's a question every one of us has to honestly answer for ourselves.

Someone else may ask, "How can we gauge whether we are serving God rather than money?" Repeat: the litmus test is in our attitude. We can obtain a quick result by answering these questions: what is my priority in life? Can I give up all my money in a hurry to serve God's purpose for my life (Matthew 19:16-23)? When the choice to make more money or attend Bible class presents itself, which one do we close the door to at the expense of the other? The truth is crystallized: any attempts to divide loyalty betray, not partial commitment to discipleship, but deep seated commitment to idolatry. The truth in 1 Timothy 6:9 remains unchanged: *"But those who want to get rich fall into temptation and a snare and many foolish and harmful desires which plunge men into ruin and destruction."*

Idolatry requires discipline. It's always a recipe for disaster, which the Supreme Court Judge administers from the eternal bar of justice! We are now ready to examine the last point of this section, namely materialism.

IDOLATRY OF MATERIALISM

Welcome to our graveyards! The graveyards of materialism! The "I want more, I want more" syndrome has buried many of us in the burial grounds of covetousness and idolatry. Who could argue that human wants are insatiable? We want this; we want that; sooner we get this; later we get that; we want this and that all over again! An endless circle of wants! Let there be no misunderstanding. There is nothing sinful about us desiring to have one thing or the other in life; it is the obsession and unquenchable passion infused in the desire itself that make us idolaters and consequently the enemies of God (James 4:4). This phenomenal insight is brought to light in the Pauline epistle to the Colossians, as previously cited: "*Therefore consider the members of your earthly body as dead to immorality, impurity, passion, evil desire, and greed, which amounts to idolatry. For it is because of these things that the wrath of God will come upon the sons of disobedience*" (Colossians 3:5-6).

Greed, which is a robust manifestation of lack of contentment, is what best describes materialism. Dr. Spiro made this sobering comment about greed: "Greed, desiring to have more than one has, not because it is insufficient but because others have more. Such desire is called 'idolatry.'"[20] The acid test of a mental attitude of materialism is a simple one: do I constantly find myself dealing with the "I want more, I want more" syndrome? If so, according to Scripture, we could be involved in whitewashed idolatry, the most subtle of all! We call it *whitewashed* because we can hardly see anything wrong about our uncontrollable lust for things, especially if we are in the position to afford them.

We said earlier that idolatry is one scripturally noted avenue whereby we ignorantly enter into worship with demons (1 Corinthians 10:19-20; Revelation 9:20). We know that Christians cannot be demon possessed; however,

---

[20] Dr. Spiro, NASB, footnote, 1995, p. 1581.

their minds can be demon influenced (2 Corinthians 6:16; 1 John 4:4; cf. 1 Timothy 4:1). But there is much more to just wanting to acquire more things in life. The obsessive passion to acquire it all is a sure sign of a heart that is devoid of spiritual vitality. It's a picture of a heart that has been deceptively coated with and influenced by demonic thinking. Much more, it's a heart that lacks the absolute peace and tranquility that God alone provides!

What is the relationship between materialism and demonism? They go hand-in-hand. We cannot ascertain the origin of materialism other than to say that it's the fruit of the sin nature and it is ancient. The relationship between the two was brought to the surface through the apostolic teaching and their vigorous attack on Gnosticism. Gnosticism "taught that body is evil, and since it is evil in itself and cannot be redeemed from its evil ways, it might as well do whatever it wants."[21] In other words, live it up! The hope is here and now! My friend, such a thought alone is evil. Essentially what materialism portrays is that we can fill up the vacuums and hollows in our souls with material things apart from God. The truth of the matter is that no one has been able to accomplish such a task and no one can apart from God. The question confronting us is, are we materialistic? Or better, how can we determine whether we are?

Ask yourself, right now, am I preoccupied with anything other than Christ my Savior? Is there anything that if I lost it today I would be devastated? Am I content with what I have, no matter how little? Can I say the following, like the apostle Paul?

---

[21] Ibid.

Not that I speak from want; for I have learned to be content in whatever circumstances I am. I know how to get along with humble means, and I also know how to live in prosperity; in any and every circumstance I have learned the secret of being filled and going hungry, both of having abundance and suffering need (Philippians 4:11-12).

If you were to lose everything like Job did, could you confidently make these words your own? *"Naked I came from my mother's womb, And naked I shall return there. The LORD gave and the LORD has taken away. Blessed be the name of the LORD"* (Job 1:21). The truth of the matter is that we cannot be materialistic and still claim to be living a spiritual life. Simply, materialism is the epitome of white-washed idolatry!

John the Apostle wrote,

Do not love the world nor the [material] things in the world. If anyone loves the world, the love of the Father is not in him. For all that is in the world, the lust of the flesh and the lust of the eyes [things we can see and covet] and the boastful pride of life, is not from the Father, but is from the world [from Satan]. And the world is passing away, and also its lusts; but the one who does the will of God lives forever (1 John 2:15-17).

In James 4:4, James, because of the enormous conse-quences of idolatry on Christendom, did not hesitate to rebuke his audience sharply: *"You adulteresses, do you not know that friendship with the world is hostility toward God? Therefore whoever wishes to be a friend of the world makes himself an enemy of God."* James is saying that we cannot eat our cake and have it too. We cannot have it both ways. When we choose material things over God, we distance ourselves from Him by virtue of our involvement in idolatry. My friend, you cannot afford to be on the opposing side of God!

In 1 Timothy 6:11, Paul, the greatest apostle the world has ever known, exhorted Timothy, *"But flee from these things, you man of God, and pursue righteousness, godliness, faith, love, perseverance, and gentleness."* And John, the last apostle, had these encouraging words for us all:

> *And we know that the Son of God has come, and has given us understanding so that we may know Him who is true; and we are in Him who is true, in His Son Jesus Christ. This is the true God and eternal life. Little children, guard yourselves from idols* (1 John 5:20-21).

That's the Word of God! Now the table is set for an in-depth examination of God's sovereignty over disaster.

6 | God's Sovereignty over Disaster

The LORD has established His throne in the heavens,
And His sovereignty rules over all (Psalm 103:19).

Recall that *sovereignty* means that the Creator-God has absolute, supreme, airtight control in everything as He directs and superintends all events of the universe in accordance with the counsel of His will (Ephesians 1:11). My friend, when we say He controls everything, we mean *everything*! Nothing is left out! His sovereignty undergirds all events of history, no matter how minute. That means no accidents or coincidences in the affairs of His Kingdom! No disaster, personal or national, will occur without His approval! That equally means that Satan cannot cause one iota of havoc in the world except when permitted by God! This should be very comforting to us who are obedient to God's plan, knowing that Satan cannot lift a finger against us without God's permission (Job 1:8-12; Luke 22:31). We shall discuss this later. But right now we want to focus on God's sovereignty in disaster. There are primarily two ways God uses disaster to keep history in check, namely indirect and direct control. Let us discuss indirect control first.

INDIRECT CONTROL

The future is as perspicuous as the past was to the sovereign, omniscient God. He knows all the knowable, including the actual and the probable. For instance, He knew what could have happened had President George W. Bush not won the election, in as much as He knew what could have happened had Al Gore won after the recount. The truth is that God does not have the human fallibility that requires us to say "Oops" when things slip through our hands. There is nothing that could ever prompt God to say "Oops"; He is in total control. We know that His ultimate goal in all He does is to bring glory to Himself; consequently, whatever He permits Satan to do, He does on the basis that the end result will glorify Him. This was exemplified in the crucifixion of our Lord Jesus Christ. God in eternity past knew the outcome of Christ's crucifixion, but Satan didn't. Satan thought that by getting rid of Christ he would bring an end to God's ultimate plan of salvation for man. Did he succeed? No! Rather, as the apostle Peter said,

> *Men of Israel, listen to these words: Jesus the Nazarene, a man attested to you by God with miracles and wonders and signs which God performed through Him in your midst, just as you yourselves know—this Man, delivered over by the **predetermined plan and foreknowledge of God**, you nailed to a cross by the hands of godless men and put Him to death. And God raised Him up again, putting an end to the agony of death, since it was impossible for Him to be held in its power...Therefore let all the house of Israel know for certain that God has made Him both Lord and Christ*

[the Savior]—this Jesus whom you crucified (Acts 2:22-36, emphasis added).

We know that God cannot be involved in any form of evil. He cannot collaborate with Satan and his minions in their evil operations. However, He is the Master in the use of the by-products of their dubious work in the accomplishments of His overall plan. What a joy to know that God is an expert in bringing a sensational result out of a hopeless situation! That knowledge should be soothing to our souls! This phenomenal truth is highlighted in Psalm 76:10, where the Psalmist wrote, *"For the wrath of man shall praise You; With a remnant of wrath You will gird Yourself."* Besides the example of Christ as we mentioned earlier, there are a thousand and more examples of God using the work of Satan and his minions to accomplish His objectives.

Joseph was another perfect example.[22] In the course of time, God made a promise to promote Joseph to a position of leadership; but because of his siblings' high-powered hatred toward him, they sold him to Egypt as a slave, hoping to end his dream of ever ruling over them (Genesis 37:18-28). That was the work of the devil! He influenced those siblings to act cold-bloodedly and pitilessly toward their brother Joseph so as to foil God's plan for Joseph. Did they succeed? Oh no! Not a chance!

Egypt was actually where God wanted Joseph to go in the first place. God used the dirty work of those callous siblings to accomplish His plan and purpose. He promoted Joseph to the position of prime minister in Egypt, thereby fulfilling His plan for the young man's life. Guess what? Thirteen years

---

[22] Moses C. Onwubiko, *Joseph, a Pillar of Grace.*

later, his siblings came and prostrated themselves before him, fulfilling his dream (Genesis 42:6). Later Joseph soothed the panic-stricken hearts of his brothers after revealing himself to them:

> *But Joseph said to them, "Do not be afraid, for am I in God's place? As for you, you meant evil against me, but God meant it for good in order to bring about this present result, to preserve many people alive. So therefore, do not be afraid; I will provide for you and your little ones." So he comforted them and spoke kindly to them* (Genesis 50:19-20).

That is a supreme illustration of Psalm 76:10: "*For the wrath of man shall praise You; With a remnant of wrath You will gird Yourself.*" Joseph's brothers "*meant evil against*" their brother in what they did, but "*God meant it for good,*" turning their evil work into a blessing for Joseph. The apostle Paul in Romans 8:28 echoed Joseph: "*And we know that God causes all things [uses everything, including the work of the evil one] to work together for good to those who love God, to those who are called according to His purpose.*" That is sovereignty! Let us say this in the simplest way: God cannot and will not allow any disaster, any disappointment, or any misfortune to take place in the affairs of His Kingdom if He knows it will not bring Him glory. It's that simple! That's what indirect control is all about!

DIRECT CONTROL

Sovereignty, as we noted, is a guarantee that the counsel of God's will, His decrees, will ultimately come to pass! Take for instance, if God has decreed that this universe will last for 20,000 years before its destruction and a new heaven and a new earth are created (2 Peter 3:10-13), He will guard it from self-destruction until His decree comes to fruition (Matthew 5:18). As any sensible parents would do to keep order in their home, God will take any measure and use any means to curtail and deter anyone, any community of people or nation, that is working contrary to His decree. We know that everything is at God's disposal; that includes tornadoes, hurricanes, scorching heat, and floods, just to name a few. Satan and his minions are God's servants too (Psalm 103:20). He can use them at will! God's plan must be fulfilled at all cost! That is what we mean when we say that God controls history.

> *Remember this, and be assured; Recall it to mind, you transgressors. Remember the former things long past, For I am God, and there is no other; I am God, and there is no one like Me, declaring the end from the beginning, and from ancient times things which have not been done, saying, 'My purpose will be established, and I will accomplish all My good pleasure'; Calling a bird of prey from the east, the man of My purpose from a far country. Truly I have spoken; truly I will bring it to pass. I have planned it, surely I will do it* (Isaiah 46:8-11).

The truth of the matter is that when God speaks, all human debates and roundtable discussions come to a screeching halt. We saw this in operation. God's decree was that the world would be populated. To this effect, He created our first parents, Adam and Eve, and commanded them to fulfill this purpose of propagating the whole planet Earth (Genesis 1:28). However, in Noah's day, evil threatened to shatter God's plan. As a result, God used the first lethal weapon of destruction on record, namely unequalled catastrophic flood, to destroy the entire human race except the righteous ones, Noah and his family, and a pair each of all other creatures (Genesis 6-9). In brief, we read from Moses' account,

> *Then the LORD saw that the wickedness of man was great on the earth, and that every intent of the thoughts of his heart was only evil continually...And the LORD said, "I [God, not Satan] will blot out man whom I have created from the face of the land, from man to animals to creeping things and to birds of the sky; for I am sorry that I have made them"* (Genesis 6:5-7).

> *It came about after the seven days, that the water of the flood came upon the earth. In the six hundredth year of Noah's life, in the second month, on the seventeenth day of the month, on the same day all the fountains of the great deep burst open, and the floodgates of the sky were opened [God created them, and He alone opened them]. The rain fell upon the earth for forty days and forty nights...The water prevailed fifteen cubits higher, and the mountains were covered. All flesh that moved on the earth perished, birds and cattle and beasts and every swarming thing that swarms upon the earth, and all mankind* (Genesis 7:10-21).

What destruction! Who was responsible? Of course, God! We see God can use any means to accomplish His purpose and still be a righteous God. Right now we use capital punishment to rid society of evil; God does the exact same thing. He uses whatever means He deems best to keep His world in check! In Noah's time, He used flood as weapon of mass destruction. Today, God, the unchanging One, still uses floods, hurricanes, and tornadoes directly or indirectly to accomplish His purpose. However, this does not mean that every disaster in life is a result of disobedience, as we saw in Job's experience. In Job's case, God gave Satan access to the "fire of God" (Job 1:16) and His wind (Job 1:19), so that he might use them as weapons of disaster against Job. We shall examine this in detail as our work progresses. We reiterate, there are no accidents in God's plan, and Satan would be jobless without a renewable and revocable case-by-case work permit from the Sovereign God. It's fascinating, indeed!

This brings us to the remaining two more examples.

Right after God began afresh with Noah's family, He repeated the same mandate that He gave to Adam and Eve, namely that they populate the world (Genesis 9:1). God wanted them to spread and cover the earth. His intention was for man's population to grow to the point where it could be grouped into nations, with national autonomy and boundaries and cultures, which undoubtedly were meant to keep evil in check. For instance, a nation can be influenced by evil through its culture, which will result in God dealing with that nation alone rather than the whole world at large. We shall get to that later. But did they listen to God's mandate? Not really. Rather, they chose to disobey His order, as we read in Genesis:

> *Now the whole earth used the same language and the same words. It came about as they journeyed east, that they found a plain in the land of Shinar and settled there. They said to one another, "Come, let us make bricks and burn them thoroughly." And they used brick for stone, and they used tar for mortar. They said, "Come, let us build for ourselves a city, and a tower*

whose top will reach into heaven, and let us make for ourselves a name, otherwise we will be scattered abroad over the face of the whole earth." The LORD came down to see the city and the tower which the sons of men had built. The LORD said, "Behold, they are one people, and they all have the same language. And this is what they began to do, and now nothing which they purpose to do will be impossible for them. Come, let Us go down and there confuse their language, so that they will not understand one another's speech." So the LORD scattered them abroad from there over the face of the whole earth; and they stopped building the city (Genesis 11:1-8).

That's right! They had a congregational meeting, and the outcome was "*Let us make for ourselves a name, otherwise we will be scattered abroad over the face of the whole earth.*" That's in total defiance of Genesis 9:1: "*Be fruitful and multiply, and fill the earth.*" What did God do in response? He used a non-lethal weapon, a disaster of a language barrier, to force them to comply. We see that God can use any means to accomplish His purpose. We have nationalities today, thanks to different languages, the fingerprints of the sovereign God! With boundaries in place, every nation can maintain its territory so that evil can be kept in check. Invariably, God administers justice on an individual and national basis, as was the case with Sodom and Gomorrah, our last example.

DESTRUCTION OF SODOM AND GOMORRAH

We know what happened to Sodom and Gomorrah and the primary reason for their total obliteration. In a nutshell, the inhabitants of that land were soaked in a pool of evil in every sense. They were involved in every kind of evil. They considered homosexuality a natural biological lifestyle, similar to what is happening in a handful of countries, including the United States of America, where civil liberty statutes have given the green light to same-sex marriage and some churches even bless such a despicable union in the eyes of God. Of course this tolerant attitude of our society was what prompted one of the revered evangelists of our day to make a heartbroken comment in view of what happened to the people of Sodom and Gomorrah, as we noted previously. His statement, of course, was based on his firm understanding of God's justice.

As George Washington and Jefferson lamented respectively, "The propitious smiles of Heaven can never be expected on a nation that disregards the eternal rules of order and right which Heaven itself [God] has ordained" (Washington), and "I tremble for my country when I reflect that God is just; and His justice cannot sleep for ever" (Jefferson).[23] Sin is like erosion and must be checked; otherwise God's purpose in creation would be thwarted before its fruition. In Sodom, the flood of evil was overrunning to the point of encroaching on its neighboring countries. It was threatening God's plan, as in Noah's time. Consequently God had to do something to curtail evil in that part of the world. We read,

> *And the LORD said, "The outcry of Sodom and Gomorrah is indeed great, and their sin is exceedingly grave."...Then the LORD rained on Sodom and Gomorrah brimstone and fire from the LORD out of heaven, and He overthrew those cities, and all the*

---

[23] William J. Federer, *America's God and Country,* 2000

valley, and all the inhabitants of the cities, and what grew on the ground (Genesis 18:20; 19:24-25).

We see God didn't use any indirect agent; He did it Himself. That's direct control! *"Then the LORD rained on Sodom and Gomorrah brimstone and fire from the LORD out of heaven, and He overthrew those cities."* My friend, let me be a little personal. It goes without saying that there is no smoke without fire. That's to say, you ought not to explain away uncontrollable suffering in your life. You ought not to explain away why all doors seem to have slammed in your face. You need not explain away why you appear to be running in circles no matter how hard you work. As a nation, we need not explain away unusual weather-related catastrophes and economic woes. We need not explain away disaster such as 9/11 by pointing fingers at one another. We need not blame anyone but ourselves. We need not shift blame to industries for contributing to the so-called global warming. God is in charge, not global warming! The compelling question then is, could it be that the Lord is trying to get our attention through all these disastrous events in our lives? *"When disaster comes to a city, has not the LORD caused it?"* (Amos 3:6, NIV; cf. Exodus 4:11).

Meditate on this question: who creates tornadoes, God? If we believed that God created everything, we would attribute their creation to God. The second question is, who controls tornadoes, God or Satan? If we believe in sovereignty, we will say God. Now here comes the mind-stimulating question: if a tornado passes through our town with a devastating result, who can we say is behind it? Well, if we say Satan, that would make us illogical thinkers! In reality, if God created it, if God is in control, we can affirm that all disasters are the handwork of God directly or indirectly! Dr. H. A. Ironside concurred:

> There are no second causes with Him. "Shall there be evil in a city, and the Lord hath not done it?" asks the prophet [Amos 3:6]... [Calamity] cannot come save as permitted by the Lord. And knowing that "all things work together for good to those who love God, who are the called according to his purpose," why should the believer either doubt or fear? Waves may roll high, stormy winds may beat tempestuously, all to which the heart had clung may seem to be swept away, but Christ abides unchanged and unchangeable, the everlasting portion of those who trust His grace.[24]

In the wake of disaster, all we are left is reflection. Yes, reflection! We shall discuss reflection in chapter 11. The real question we should ask ourselves in the aftermath of disaster is, what message is God endeavoring to convey to us? This question and more shall be answered in the upcoming chapter.

---

[24] H. A. Ironside, *Philippians* (Baltimore, Maryland: Loizeaux, 1922, revised 1997), p. 48.

7 | Decoding God's Message in Disaster

And for many days Israel was without the true God and without a teaching priest and without law. But in their distress they turned to the LORD God of Israel, and they sought Him, and He let them find Him. In those times there was no peace to him who went out or to him who came in, for many disturbances afflicted all the inhabitants of the lands. Nation was crushed by nation, and city by city, for God troubled them with every kind of distress (2 Chronicles 15:3-6).

Ironically, every disaster in life is coded with a message that requires discernment, reflection and wisdom to decode, a subject we shall look into later on in our study. As we mentioned in our introduction, disaster as far as God is concerned is nothing but a bell. It could be a bell of warning or a bell of preparation for spiritual refinement. In the olden days and even today, in most third-world countries, community bells are used for several purposes. They are used as public time clock. There are bells of joy when there is a new birth or something that calls for jubilation. There are bells of mourning when there is a death in the village. Furthermore, they are used in emergency situations and to alert people for war.

Going back to the time of Ezekiel, the people of his day knew too well about this system, as his book reveals:

And the word of the LORD came to me, saying, "Son of man, speak to the sons of your people and say to them, 'If I [God] bring a sword upon a land [by way of a disaster], and the people of the land take one man from among them and make him their watchman, and he sees the sword [of disaster] coming upon the land and blows on the trumpet [or rings a bell] and warns the people, then he who hears the sound of the trumpet [or bell] and does not take warning, and a sword comes and takes him away, his blood will be on his own head. He heard the sound of the trumpet but did not take warning; his blood will be on himself. But had he taken warning [taken God's warning bell seriously], he would have delivered his life. But if the watchman sees the sword coming and does not blow the trumpet, and the people are not warned, and [God's] sword comes and takes a person from them, he is taken away in his iniquity; but his blood I will require from the watchman's hand'" (Ezekiel 33:1-6).

We shall comment on this passage, but before we do, we need to consider the obvious challenge of decoding the hidden message in a bell. I remember vividly, when I was growing up, we had a bell in our village, which served four purposes. It alerted people to a time for worship. It was used in an emergency situation to gather the men of the village in the village square in a matter of minutes. It was used as a time clock. Finally, it was used as a mourning bell when there was a death in the village. The challenge for us, as it is for all who rely on this communication system, is that of being able to decipher every bell tone. I learned that it only took hearing a pattern of rings once to interpret it. For instance, if there was a death, one would hear perhaps a dozen rings at intervals of ninety seconds each. Soon, everyone would be asking, "Who died?" God in His infinite wisdom uses the bell of disaster in a similar fashion. We hear God's bells almost every day.

However, the problem with many of us is threefold. The first problem is that we are too busy to sit down and decipher each pattern. The second is that we are quick to explain away the warning bells of disaster from a humanistic viewpoint rather than see it from God's viewpoint. The third is that we often ignore the tones outright.

The purpose of this book is to sound a warning to all of us. Every communicator ought to take notice of God's Word through Ezekiel. We are responsible to sound God's alarm in our generation! As ambassadors, we are responsible to share God's message with those in our periphery. We are responsible to let people know that *the justice of God cannot sleep forever.*

We had already noted the implication of God's sovereignty, namely, that nothing ever happens in the universe apart from His sovereign will and purpose. Consequently, every disaster, no matter the magnitude, has a hidden code of God's signature (Amos 3:6). Every disaster, such as a car wreck, a cyclone, Hurricane Katrina, 9/11, or an earthquake is a messenger from on high. That's what the Bible says! "*He makes the winds His messengers, Flaming fire His ministers*" (Psalm 104:4; cf. 148:8; 107:33-35).

To whom does God send His messages? His messages reach three types of people: the unsaved, reckless believers, and God's obedient children. No one is exempt! No one is exempt from disaster; the spiritual, the carnal, and the unsaved—all share in one form of disaster or another.

GOD'S MESSAGE TO THE UNSAVED

Thomas Jefferson, in his address to the State of Virginia, made this startling statement: "I tremble for my country when I reflect that God is just; that His justice cannot sleep forever." God, in His infinite mercy, longsuffering, righteousness and justice, has a limit to how far He can let us go in our evil ways before He rains judgment on us. He extends to us ample grace before judgment. However, if we continue to ignore His grace overture, sooner or later His justice takes over: *"The LORD tests the righteous and the wicked, And the one who loves violence His soul hates. Upon the wicked He will rain snares; Fire and brimstone and burning wind will be the portion of their cup"* (Psalm 11:5-6).

Of course, the hidden message from God is that we need to examine our own lives in light of eternity. In essence, the warning bell is telling us, "Time is running out; make peace with God through Jesus Christ before it's too late!" It's telling us to heed His message of hope through the gospel and thus pursue the path of spiritual integrity by means of intake and application of sound Bible teaching. Scriptures abound with references to people who embraced God's grace through disaster.

King Nebuchadnezzar is a perfect example of those whom the Lord humbled through the hidden message of a disaster. God used a disaster of insanity that left him totally devastated in the wilderness for seven years until he acknowledged God's grace (Daniel 4:28-37). Saul of Tarsus before his conversion is another example. Over and over he ignored God's invitation to embrace His grace through faith alone in

Christ alone (Acts 7-8:1-3). He too stiffened his neck, until the Lord from on High blasted his sight with the light of His glory, which compelled him to change his course (Acts 9:1-16). That's grace!

My friend, there is no better way for God to convey His love toward us as unbelievers than through disasters piled on top of one another! You ask, "Why is that?" The truth is that if God could get your attention through unsurpassing difficulties, which in turn causes you to put your trust in His Son, He has done the most for you, ever! For eternity in the lake of fire is beyond the scope of this book. The thought alone sends chills through my spines!

But again, there are those who experience disasters, one after another, and still refuse to obey God, Pharaoh being an example. But there's no reason for you to resist the Almighty. There is no reason to continue in disobedience until it's too late, as it was for the rich man that the Lord told us about (Luke 16:19-31). Gambling with your eternal destiny is the worst kind of gamble, period. The truth of the matter is that once death catches up with you without Christ, your hope of spending eternity with God is forever dashed (Hebrews 9:27). You shouldn't let anyone fool you by telling you that hope awaits you if you should die without Christ.

The Roman Catholic church teaches about purgatory, alleging that if an individual dies without Christ, God will punish the individual for a period of time and then transfer the individual to Heaven. That's a false hope! It is not scriptural at all! Scripture is crystal clear on this: "*And inasmuch as it is appointed for men to die once and after this comes judgment*" (Hebrews 9:27; cf. Luke 16:19-31).

We are now ready to examine the next group.

RECKLESS BELIEVERS

I deliberately chose the word *reckless*. Obviously we wreck our lives when we take our spiritual lives for granted. We wreck our lives when we live a mediocre spiritual life. We wreck our lives when all we do is show up in a Bible class and take good notes but never allow the teaching of His Word to influence our thinking and action. The apostle Paul had a word of caution to Timothy and us, saying,

> *But realize [take note of] this, that in the last days difficult times will come. For men will be lovers of self, lovers of money, boastful, arrogant, revilers, disobedient to parents, ungrateful, unholy, unloving, irreconcilable, malicious gossips, without self-control, brutal, haters of good, treacherous,* **reckless***, conceited, lovers of pleasure rather than lovers of God; holding to a form of godliness [for example, by regularly showing up in Bible class], although they have denied its power; Avoid such men as these. For among them are those who enter into households [of God] and captivate weak women weighed down with sins, led on by various impulses, always learning and never able to come to the knowledge of the truth [to the point of allowing the Word to influence their thinking]* (2 Timothy 3:1-7, emphasis added).

My friend, sooner or later God will say, "Enough is enough; it's time for a messenger of disaster!"

> *The LORD, the God of their fathers, sent word to them again and again by His messengers, because He had compassion on His people and on His dwelling place; but they continually mocked the messengers of God,*

despised His words and scoffed at His prophets, until the wrath of the LORD arose against His people, until there was no remedy (2 Chronicles 36:15-16).

And you have [quickly] forgotten the exhortation which is addressed to you as sons, "My son, do not regard lightly the discipline of the Lord, nor faint when you are reproved by Him; for those whom the Lord loves He disciplines, and He scourges [afflicts] every son whom He receives" (Hebrews 12:5-6).

What better way to illustrate these passages than to consult the story of the prodigal son. The prodigal son began his journey as a son in a wealthy family and along the way through bad decisions wrecked his life. The Bible tells us that pleasure was more important to him than his relationship with his father, which caused him to rebel against his father's daily instructions and care. His choice of pleasure drove him out into the world, where pleasure abounded. The Father visited him with disaster in his reckless lifestyle until He backed him into a corner (Luke 15:14-16)!

But when he came to his senses [through reflection], he said, "How many of my father's hired men have more than enough bread, but I am dying here with hunger! I will get up and go to my father, and will say to him, 'Father, I have sinned against heaven, and in your sight; I am no longer worthy to be called your son; make me as one of your hired men'" (Luke 15:17-19).

We know that the prodigal son represents a believer by virtue of his position as a son in the family and because he knows that he is out of fellowship. He literally exemplifies what a reckless believer is all about. A hidden bell of disaster is God's chosen recourse to relay His message of displeasure with him in regard to his reckless lifestyle (Psalm 119:67,71). This clears the table for our next examination.

GOD'S OBEDIENT CHILDREN

Who can they be but those who love God? They are believers in Christ who diligently learn and apply God's Word daily, to the glory of God. To them, living is Christ, dying is Christ (Philippians 1:21; cf. Romans 14:8). Guess what? They too are not disaster-proof! They are not free from suffering! But they never view disaster as a divine discipline but rather as a blessing in disguise. They consider it an honor that the sovereign, omnipotent God has considered them worthy to be enrolled in the elite college of suffering, where they will further learn how to totally rely on God and be of good service to Him. Here they are trained in how to maximize God's divine provision, namely, His Word and the fruit of His Spirit (Galatians 5:22). Through suffering they are trained to be proficient in handling the shield of faith (Ephesians 6:13-16, cf. Hebrews 5:13-14). My beloved, that's grace in disguise!

Can we think of anyone who best fits this profile of a righteous one who suffered? Job, of course! He is described as a man of spiritual integrity, whose spiritual life is unequalled (Job 1:1,8); and yet, with the exception of the God-Man Jesus Christ, Job experienced disaster like no other. We ask, "What's the essence of suffering for God's obedient children?" Scripture has the answer: "*Although He [Jesus Christ] was a Son, He learned obedience from the things which He suffered. And having been made perfect, He became to all those who obey [trust in] Him the source of eternal salvation*" (Hebrews 5:8-9). Suffering, then, is part and parcel of God's amazing plan for His children. He uses suffering to aid us in developing spiritual tenacity. Think of it: the righteous One, who has no iota of sin in Him, still goes through the furnace of suffering. That's a mystery! But the sublime truth is that every believer in good standing experiences suffering for blessing (Philippians 1:29; cf. John 16:33).

"Consider it all joy, my brethren, when you encounter various trials, knowing that the testing of your faith produces endurance. And let endurance have its perfect result, so that you may be perfect and complete, lacking in nothing" (James 1:2-4). God's ultimate purpose is to mature us. He wants His very best for His obedient children (Psalm 34:10; 84:11). Suffering, then, is God's vehicle that drives us along His highway of blessing. There are no two ways about it! That explains why Job said, *"But He knows the way I take; when He has tried me, I shall come forth as gold* [purified]*"* (Job 23:10). Of course, he did shine brighter than before, to the glory of the Almighty (Job 42:10-17)! *"Blessed is a man who perseveres under trial; for once he has been approved* [tested and passed]*, he will receive the crown of life which the Lord has promised to those who love Him"* (James 1:12).

This raises an important question, namely, what's the difference between divine discipline and suffering for blessing?

Scripture has the answer. Divine discipline makes one totally uncomfortable. It comes with intolerable and unbearable shooting pain! All spiritual tranquilizers are removed from us, or rather, because of our reckless life, we have removed ourselves from divine power. We have no peace, no joy, and no patience, the by-products of the Holy Spirit, to help us deal with the disaster in our lives. Above all, we wreck the pipeline of His Word to our soul, and hence we cannot think in terms of doctrinal rationale. In the final analysis, we are miserable! Tragically, some have even ended their lives because of the intensity of such suffering.

But a disaster that is tailored for blessing does not cause havoc in the soul; nor does it hamper a believer's inner tranquility. He has access to joy, peace, patience, and longsuffering (Galatians 5:22-23). These keep the believer vibrant in this time of testing.

Let's look at two believers who received an avalanche of disasters in their lifetimes, one as a discipline and the other as a blessing in disguise. We know about King David's ultimate spiritual failure, how his sin of adultery, hypocrisy, and murder ruptured his fellowship with God. Eventually, God in His grace got his attention through unbearable suffering, as he himself explained:

> *When I kept silent about my sin [when I ignored it outright], my body wasted away Through my groaning all day long. For day and night Your hand was heavy upon me [with divine discipline]; My vitality was drained away as with the fever heat of summer [no spiritual energy]* (Psalm 32:3-4).

> *O LORD, rebuke me not in Your wrath, And chasten me not in Your burning anger. For Your arrows [of disaster] have sunk deep into me, And Your hand has pressed down on me. There is no soundness in my flesh because of Your indignation; There is no health in my bones because of my sin. For my iniquities are gone over my head; As a heavy burden they weigh too much for me. My wounds grow foul and fester Because of my folly. I am bent over and greatly bowed down; I go mourning all day long. For my loins are filled with*

burning, And there is no soundness in my flesh. I am benumbed and badly crushed [by the finger of God]; I groan because of the agitation of my heart [unbearable suffering]...My heart throbs, my strength fails me; And the light of my eyes, even that has gone from me. My loved ones and my friends stand aloof from my plague; And my kinsmen stand afar off. Those who seek my life lay snares for me; and those who seek to injure me have threatened destruction, And they devise treachery all day long (Psalm 38:1-12).

Therein is a perfect illustration of unbearable suffering! King David, like the prodigal son, had no spiritual power available to him. The pipeline of God's Word to his soul was clogged up! What a contrast! The same person who used doctrinal rationale when face-to-face with Goliath (1 Samuel 17:47) is a totally different person now. Of course, God in His infinite wisdom had to send David a message through suffering.

What about Job? His suffering, unlike David's, was a suffering for blessing. But how did he handle it? With poise! With divine viewpoint thinking! Let us examine some of his doctrinal thinking when disaster hit him right between the eyes. After a long list of disasters were reported, he said, *"Naked I came from my mother's womb, And naked I shall return there. The LORD gave and the LORD has taken away. Blessed be the name of the LORD"* (Job 1:21).

Though He slay me, I will hope in Him (Job 13:15).

But He knows the way I take; When He has tried me, I shall come forth as gold. My foot has held fast to His path; I have kept His way and not turned aside. I have not departed from the command of His lips; I have treasured the words of His mouth more than my necessary food (Job 23:10-12).

And as for me, I know that my Redeemer lives, And at the last He will take His stand on the earth. Even after my skin is destroyed, Yet from my flesh I shall see God (Job 19:25-26).

What an obedient believer! What a demonstration of the dynamic power of the Word of God, even in dark times! What a comfort to know, like Job, that though God slays His obedient children through disaster, He will see them through when His purpose is completed. That's exactly why James exhorts us, saying, *"Consider it all joy, my brethren, when you encounter various trials, knowing that the testing of your faith produces endurance. And let endurance have its perfect result, that you may be perfect and complete, lacking in nothing"* (James 1:2-4).

We have just considered how God communicates to all of us by way of disaster. We are now ready to examine, in the next chapter, national disasters and see what kind of warning bell they serve in a nation.

8 | Warning Bell of National Disaster

We begin by asking ourselves, what are the primary roots of a national disaster? We have already mentioned idolatry. We shall offer other reasons later on in our study. But before then, let's consider a nation at large. It goes without saying that a tree does not make a forest; similarly, an individual does not constitute a nation. It takes a group of trees to form a forest and likewise a group of people to form a nation. Sequentially, then, the circle of a nation starts with a couple, then a family, a community, and a full-blown nation. Simplified, a couple is the lifeline of a family, and its status quo in any given time directly and indirectly affects an entire family and a nation at large. Make no mistake! An unhealthy marriage is a catalyst that kicks off a chain reaction that cumulates and results in a national breakdown. It explains why God takes marriage seriously! "*Marriage is to be held in honor among all, and the marriage bed is to be undefiled; for fornicators and adulterers God will judge*" (Hebrews 13:4). That's the Word of God, and God keeps His Word! I echo the words of Tom Elliff, the former Southern Baptist Convention president: "A society that doesn't value the institution of marriage is a society headed toward destruction, which can already be noted in the way many children from broken homes perform once outside those homes."[25] This is true of every nation! Marriage is not the focal point of our study; we already have written a book on it, *Focus on Christian Marriage*.[26] We simply invoke marriage to demonstrate that a bad marriage inevitably brews sour wine in a family, which in turn sours the entire society from cradle to grave. Obviously, when there's a breakdown in marriage, children pay heavily!

While a couple is the lifeline of a family, children are the lifeline of a society, and God takes the issue of raising them seriously! It makes more sense to us when we read afresh the words of King Solomon, the wisest man who ever lived: *"Train up a child in the way he should go, Even when he is old he will not depart from it"* (Proverbs 22:6). There are no "ifs" or "buts" about it. We can either pay the price of training our children now and have a blessed harvest in the distant future or we can delay the cost and pay heavily with tears later. Tragically, it appears that many of us parents are already in the harvest field with tears.

We all know too well that home is where a nation is conceived, incubated, hatched, nurtured, and carved out as parents sacrifice all in child-rearing. The state of children is important, not only in the family, but also outside the family. Often we miscalculate the consequences of unruly children in a community. Think of what is happening in America today. Unruly children rule everywhere. They rule at home, in schools, and in society at large. School violence is just one way they manifest their dominance. Who was not in shock in

---

[25] Tom Elliff, *Baptist Press*, 2005.

[26] Moses C. Onwubiko, *Focus on Christian Marriage*.

April 2007, when thirty-two young students lay dead at Virginia Tech because a gunman went on the rampage on the campus? What about other school shootings, like Columbine, Georgia, California, Pennsylvania, Wisconsin, Minnesota, and Texas, just to name a few? Unruly children out of control? Those are just incidents in schools; what about violence in shopping malls and other places? It boils down to this: innocent lives are wasted daily, which makes a strong case for a divine judgment! Simply, ill-disciplined, naughty children can be terrors in a nation, which in turn begs for national disasters from the eternal bar of justice!

Suffice it to say, when it comes to equipping children to be well-mannered adults of tomorrow, home is an incubator; all others, though equally essential, such as local churches, schools, and military bases, are simply field camps. We shall elaborate on two of these subsidiary training camps, namely churches and schools, as we progress in our study. The undeniable truth, however, is that a child who is deprived of the sweet taste of home discipline is always at the mercy of God's grace wherever the individual may wind up in life. In essence, a delinquent child is a time bomb that only God can defuse. This, of course, is accomplished when the individual accepts the free gift of God, through faith alone in Christ alone, and subsequently avails himself of the teaching of the life-changing Word of God (Romans 12:2; cf. John 6:63). Let's consider home as the primary training camp.

HOME SWEET HOME

There is debate on this! Home is a launching base where children are brought up and sent forth to make up the chemistry of a society. It's where parents sacrifice time and money in order to train their children to add to the equation of peace, both at home and in society (Proverbs 29:17). Children excrete what they eat; by the same token, they regurgitate what they have learned by way of observation. Action is the most powerful teaching aid in a child's world! Parental conduct is the first gospel children read before they are able to read the Gospels of Matthew, Mark, Luke, and John. Do we teach our children both in action and words? Are we teaching them anything at all? Whatever we sow in our children, that we shall reap at harvest time (Galatians 6:7). God in His infinite wisdom has given us the tools necessary to get our job done in a manner that will honor Him. In the laws of divine establishment, God ordained parents as the heads of a household as far as children are concerned. He followed it up with a divine mandate to children: *"Honor your father and your mother, that your days may be prolonged in the land which the LORD your God gives you"* (Exodus 20:12). Make no mistake: this is the only commandment with a promise. Why is that? Children are the parents of tomorrow, the hope of a nation. We know that incorrigible children, who remain in a state of anarchy, are without hope and a future. That's to say that the lifespan of disobedient children is not worth discussing. Simply put, God's justice stands on guard to shower blessing on the children who adhere to His mandates and are obedient to their parents. By the same token, His justice is ever ready to lower the boom of disaster on those who disregard His Word, as seen in the book of Proverbs: *"When the wicked increase, transgression increases; But the righteous will see their fall"* (Proverbs 29:16). God takes the matter of children's delinquency seriously, to the point that in the Old Testament He instituted a system of capital punishment whereby delinquent children were purged from Israel's camp. The Bible tells us,

If any man has a stubborn and rebellious son who will not obey his father or his mother, and when they chastise him, he will not even listen to them, then his father and mother shall seize him, and bring him out to the elders of his city at the gateway of his hometown. They shall say to the elders of his city, "This son of ours is stubborn and rebellious, he will not obey us, he is a glutton and a drunkard." Then all the men of his city shall stone him to death; so you shall remove the evil from your midst, and all Israel shall hear of it and fear (Deuteronomy 21:18-21).

Scary thought! But hold it! Who instituted the above law? That's right, God! Several centuries later, God's Word was reiterated through the pen of King Solomon: "*He who curses his father or his mother, his lamp will go out in time of darkness*" (Proverbs 20:20). This is the Word of God!

What if the congress of the United States of America should enact such a law nowadays? How many of our children would still be alive? A handful, no doubt! You say, "Thank God, we don't have such a law!" I say, not so fast! God still administers justice in one way or another, in spite of man's failure.

Look around you today; how many delinquent children can you count on your fingers who are remarkably doing well in life, especially in dark times? I say none! On the contrary, difficult times come as a punishment to a society where incorrigible children dominate and reign supreme.

One may ask, "What about shattered homes? Yes, broken marriages make the task of rearing obedient children very difficult. That's why God vehemently said, "*I hate divorce*" (Malachi 2:16). God is acutely aware of the devastating

131

impact of divorce on children. Let's be realistic! Why is everyone in America crying that untamed children are taking over their society? The answer is not far-fetched when the divorce rate in America is computed! Let us for a moment take a close look at divorce rate in America.

DIVORCE RATE IN AMERICA

Heartbreakingly, the divorce rate in America today has reached all-time high. Tom Elliff correctly made the assertion that "America has become saturated in a 'divorce culture.'"[27] Some researchers believe that more than "50 percent of all marriages in America end up in divorce." One researcher went a step further in cataloguing the divorce rate statistically: First time married, 50 percent; second time, 67 percent; and third time, 74 percent.[28] That's not all! It was even broken down to a daily average, which amounts to about 3,571 divorces. That's 3,571 shattered homes in America every day! Elliff couldn't have said it better: "Any breakup of a marriage is a funeral of a home, which is something more Christians need to take seriously." He added, "It's one thing to grieve over 3,000 people who died in the World Trade Center, and I did over that, but if that day was like every other day in America, more than that many homes died."[29] Who can argue that a disaster in a marriage is a disaster in the chemistry of rearing up of children? How our children have fallen by the wayside of shattered homes! When we add up all this, we can clearly trace the root of

---

[27] Elliff, *Baptist Press,* 2005.

[28] Jennifer Baker, Forest Institute of Professional Psychology in Springfield, Missouri.

[29] Elliff, *Baptist Press,* 2005.

national disaster. But there's hope when children are brought up in the fear of God.

GOD—THE CENTER OF LIFE

A profound knowledge of the Creator-God is the beginning of a well balanced life, and when God is *not* in the center, things fall apart. King Solomon at one point had a spiritual relapse. In his condition, he devoted his time and money to a frantic search for happiness, but all to no avail. When he recovered from his reckless and costly experiment, his words of advice were sobering:

> *The words of wise men are like goads, and masters of these collections are like well-driven nails; they are given by one Shepherd. But beyond this, my son, be warned: the writing of many books is endless, and excessive devotion to books is wearying to the body. The conclusion, when all has been heard, is: fear God and keep His commandments, because this applies to every person* (Ecclesiastes 12:11-13).

The Psalmist agreed: "*The fear of the LORD is the beginning of wisdom; A good understanding have all those who do His commandments; His praise endures forever*" (Psalm 111:10). There can be no debate about this! A child who is brought up in the fear of God is a child whose lamp will never go out, even in hard times (Proverbs 3; Psalm 1:1-3). What can we say! God knew the impact of His Word on children, that's why He commanded through Moses, saying,

> "*You [parents] shall therefore impress these words of mine on your heart and on your soul; and you shall bind them as a sign on your hand, and they shall be as frontals on your forehead. You shall teach them to*

your sons, talking of them when you sit in your house and when you walk along the road and when you lie down and when you rise up [principle of repetition]. You shall write them on the doorposts of your house and on your gates [so that they can be read over and over and over], so that your days and the days of your sons may be multiplied on the land which the LORD swore to your fathers to give them, as long as the heavens remain above the earth" (Deuteronomy 11:18-21).

We reiterate: when God is removed from a home, it will ultimately spell out disaster in that household; and its ripple effect will resound from that home down the streets of society. A non-God-fearing home is a time bomb waiting to explode. This brings up the issue of the church in society.

THE ROLE OF A LOCAL CHURCH

A Bible-based church is not just a meeting place; it is a house of impartation of a spiritual living organism, namely God's unchanging, life-giving Word, which is so vital for the life of a society. I carefully chose the words *Bible-based* because not all local churches meet the biblical criteria, just as not all that glitters is gold. A church is a place of inculcation and reinforcement, which are the basic laws of pedagogy, the science of teaching. It reinforces the fundamental biblical truth that parents teach their children at home. More than that, it goes beyond the basics to advanced truth, which is essential for healthy living and productivity in a society (2 Timothy 3:16-17). Simply stated, a Bible-based church is a training camp for a wholesome community, in that it teaches its audience that a relationship with God is the key for healthy living, harmonious rapport in marriage, friendship, and tolerance! Consequently an explosion in a church fragments homes and society and eventually shatters a nation.

Historically we can trace the impact of the Church all the way back to the rise and fall of Rome. Edward Gibbon (1737-1794) wrote,

> If a man were called to fix the period in the history of the world during which the condition of the human race was most happy and prosperous, he would, without hesitation, name that which elapsed from the death of Domitian to the accession of Commodus. The vast extent of the Roman Empire was governed by absolute power, under the guidance of virtue and wisdom.[30]

But guess what? This was a period when the church was on fire for the Lord! Bible-based churches of the apostolic era and their products, namely spiritual-minded believers, shaped the golden age of the Roman world. That's exactly what the Bible says: "*Righteousness exalts a nation*" (Proverbs 14:34)!

> Further, it has been remarked with more ingenuity than truth that the virgin purity of the church was never violated by schism or heresy before the reign of Trajan or Hadrian, about one hundred years after the death of Christ. We may observe with much more propriety that, during that period, the disciples of the Messiah were indulged in a freer latitude both of

---

[30] Edward Gibbon, *The Decline and Fall of the Roman Empire* (New York: Harcourt, Brace and Company, 1960), p. 90.

faith and practice than has ever been allowed in succeeding ages.[31]

When the church collapsed, the balloon of spiritual integrity was deflated and air was let out of the empire gradually, and eventually the empire collapsed altogether. Ironically, it's said that Rome was not built in a day; neither was its fall.

Great Britain has a similar history. Christianity changed the British chemistry of dominance and power influence in the world. Amazingly, when Christianity came to its soil, it came with a gospel and the Bible in Latin. That soon changed, when in 1538, "Henry VIII issued a proclamation ordering 'one book of the whole Bible of the largest volume in English' to be placed in every church in England." He also ordered that it be placed where all could read it, ordering the clergy "that you shall discourage no man from reading or hearing of the said Bible but you shall expressly stir, provoke and exhort every person to read the same."[32]

"With the translation of the Bible into English and its adoption as the highest authority for an autonomous English Church, the history, traditions, and moral law of the Hebrew nation became part of the English culture; became for a period of three centuries the most powerful single influence on that culture."[33] "It became "the national epic of Britain."[34] "Everyone knew it. In many homes, it was the

---

[31] Ibid., p. 501.

[32] Barbara W. Tuchman, *Bible and Sword* (New York: Ballantine Books, 1956), p. 80.

[33] Ibid., p. 80.

[34] Thomas Huxley, quoted in Tuchman, *Bible and Sword*, p. 81.

only book in the house and, being so, was read over and over until its words and images and characters and stories became as familiar as bread. Children learned long chapters by heart."[35] What a period in the history of Great Britain! Its impact on the nation was beyond computation! But again, the death of the Church in Britain was the defining moment for its memorial service as the empire of the world.

THE DEATH OF CHURCH IN GREAT BRITAIN

Britain has been in spiritual turmoil for quite some time now. A headline in the newspaper *USA Today* captured my attention: "Is God dead in Europe?"[36] The article went on to say, "Western Europe, the cradle of modern Christianity, has become a 'post-Christian society' in which the ruling class and cultural leaders are anti-religious or 'Christophobic.'" The same newspaper released a survey of church attendance both in Europe and America. Guess what? We are almost running neck-in-neck! Thirty-three percent of Christians in America say that they attend church services or synagogues at least once a week, and in Europe, 32 percent claim to attend the same more than once a month.[37] You read it correctly! Only 33 percent of Christians in America go to church every Sunday!

Sadly, Britain has unglued itself from the spiritual glue

---

[35] Tuchman, *Bible and Sword*, p. 83.

[36] George Weigel, *The Cube and the Cathedral: Europe, America, and Politics Without God*, quoted in James P. Gannon, "Is God dead in Europe?" *USA Today*, Monday, January 9, 2006.

[37] James P. Gannon, "Is God dead in Europe?" *USA Today*, Monday, January 9, 2006, http://www.usatoday.com/news/opinion/editorials/2006-01-08-faith-edit_x.htm.

DISASTER: GOD'S WARNING BELL

that held the empire together for centuries. Our missionary team was in England in 2006. What we saw as we walked through the streets was disheartening. It broke our hearts to see an empire that once dominated the world, an empire that once ruled the world with the gospel of Jesus Christ, in a dried-up spiritual condition. We saw some of the mighty cathedrals of old being converted into condominiums and offices. Imagine! The once God-ordained incubators of spiritual giants like Charles Spurgeon are now being converted into homes and offices for the "post-Christian society." No wonder why many don't enjoy living in England anymore as they did in the olden days. "Is God dead in Europe?" If so, what effect does it have in England? Far-reaching! What about America? Is God about to die in America? If so, not without consequences! Perhaps that explains many unprecedented national disasters. They are God's warning bells! The truth is that no individual or nation can expel God from their lives and at the same time expect a cordial evening cookout! "The propitious smiles of Heaven can never be expected on a nation that disregards the eternal rules of order and right which Heaven itself [God] has ordained"[38] (George Washington). This prepares us to examine the next training camp, school.

ROLE OF SCHOOL IN A SOCIETY

School is nothing but a training camp where children are educated in every sense of the word. It's where their orientation to authority is fine-tuned. It is not just a place where children are taught math and writing skills and the like but also where mannerisms and etiquette are heightened for the good

---

[38] William J. Federer, *America's God and Country*, 2000.

of students and society. Of course, to accomplish all this, students must be taught to respect their Creator-God; for therein is the beginning of success (Proverbs 15:33).

Looking back, it's apparent that the founding fathers of America were acutely aware of the importance of making God the center of students' lives, for they overwhelmingly endorsed the book *McGuffey's Reader* by William Holmes McGuffey (1800-1873) as a cornerstone, so to say, in all schools. In fact, his work had such a profound effect on students that he was considered "the schoolmaster of the nation." His book was "the mainstay in public education in America till 1920. As of 1963, 125 million copies had been sold, making it one of the most widely used and influential textbooks of all times."[39] In its foreword, McGuffey wrote, "The Christian religion is the religion of our country. From it are derived our prevalent notions of the character of God, the great moral governor of the universe. On its doctrines are founded the peculiarities of our free institutions."[40] McGuffey's book taught students the importance of prayer, the consequences of alcoholism, and much more. His book had an indelible mark on students across the nation for over a century. But that's not all! Prior to his work, the Continental Congress had already, in 1782, authorized that Bibles be printed as "a neat edition of the Holy Scriptures for the use of schools."[41] That's right, "for the use of schools"!

---

[39] William J. Federer, *America's God and Country: Encyclopedia of Quotations* (St Louis Mo: Amerisearch, Inc., 2000), p. 439.

[40] William Holmes McGuffey, *McGuffey's Reader*, quoted in Federer, *America's God and Country*, p. 439.

[41] Ibid., p. 25.

Students were taught the role of God in life. In schools, the Bible was their manual for the true meaning and purpose of life.

What about some prestigious educational institutions in America? Interestingly, Harvard University, the first institution (1636), was founded for the primary purpose of training "a literate clergy."[42] Its students' handbook had this rule:

> Let every student be plainly instructed, and earnestly pressed to consider well, the maine end of his life and studies is, to know God and Jesus Christ which is eternall life, John 17:3 and therefore to lay Christ in the bottome, as the only foundation of all sound knowledge and Learning. And seeing the Lord only giveth wisedome, Let every one seriously set himself by prayer in secret to seeke it of him Prov. 2, 3.[43]

Equally interesting was that 106 of the first 108 schools in America were founded on the Christian faith.[44] Yale (1701) had an almost identical policy for its students. The requirements for the students included: "All scholars shall live religious, godly, and blameless lives according to the rules of God's Word, diligently reading the Holy Scriptures, the fountain of light and truth; and constantly attend upon all the duties of religion, both in public and secret.[45] Princeton University (1746) was no exception. The university's official motto was "Under God's Power She Flourishes."[46] We could

---

[42] Ibid., p. 280.

[43] Ibid., p. 281.

[44] Ibid., p. 281-282.

[45] Ibid., p. 708.

[46] Ibid., p. 520.

go on and on, but that will lead us into another subject all together. Simply, when any learning institution is set up in such a way that students are deprived of exposure to the knowledge of the true God, sooner or later it will become a student bomb-manufacturing institution. Consider public schools in America today!

Don't get me wrong. It doesn't mean that a respect for God's Word in a society will make that society perfect. I couldn't have agreed more with Francis A. Schaeffer, one of the foremost evangelical thinkers of the twenty century:

> People have never carried out the biblical teaching perfectly. Nonetheless, wherever the biblical teaching has gone, even though it has always been marred by men, it not only has told of an open approach to God through the work of Christ, but also has brought peripheral results in society, including political institutions.[47]

He added, "To whatever degree a society allows the teaching of the Bible to bring forth its natural conclusions, it is able to have form and freedom in society and government."[48]

The bulk of this chapter can be summed up in this paragraph: indifference of a society to God's Word, a high rate of marriage collapse, uncontrollable child delinquency, apathy to local churches, and diminished value in school system accumulate as the primary roots of national breakdown. In return, God sends a message of His dissatisfaction to that

---

[47] Francis A. Schaeffer, *How Should We Then Live? The Rise and Decline of Western Thought and Culture* (Wheaton, Illinois: Crossway Books, 2005), p. 105.

[48] Ibid., p. 110.

nation with regard to its way of life by means of warning bells of terrorism, unusual earthquakes, high-powered tornadoes, hurricanes, devastating floods, just to name a few of His messengers. These are national disasters! We cannot afford to ignore the infallible Word of God: "*Behold, the Lord has a strong and mighty agent; As a storm of hail, a tempest of destruction, Like a storm of mighty overflowing waters, He has cast it down to the earth with His hand*" (Isaiah 28:2). "*Therefore, thus says the Lord GOD, 'I will make a violent wind break out in My wrath. There will also be in My anger a flooding rain and hailstones to consume it in wrath'*" (Ezekiel 13:13). "*If a trumpet is blown in a city will not the people tremble? If a calamity occurs in a city has not the LORD done it?*" (Amos 3:6).

To further illustrate our points about national disaster, we shall use the next chapter to discuss national disaster in relation to God's sovereignty.

9 | God's Warning Bell in Judah

This section will throw a beam of light on how God deals with a nation. As we dig deep into our work, sooner or later light will be ignited; then we shall see clearly without a shadow of a doubt that God rules supreme. Further, we shall come to grip with the saying that Jesus Christ controls history. The chapter shall also serve as a prototype and a foundation on which we shall lay other nations as building blocks in relation to the interpretation of the justice of God as He administers justice nation by nation. As we prepare to dive in, we begin by examining God's love, mercy, longsuffering and justice, echoed loud through the voice of Jeremiah saying,

> *The LORD, the God of their fathers, sent word to them again and again by His messengers, because He had compassion on His people and on His dwelling place; but they continually mocked the messengers of God, despised His words and scoffed at His prophets, until the wrath of the LORD arose against His people, until there was no remedy. Therefore He* **[God] brought up against them the king of the Chaldeans who slew their young men with the sword** *in the house of their sanc-*

tuary, and had no compassion on young man or virgin, old man or infirm; **He [God] gave them all into his hand** (2 Chronicles 36:15-17, emphasis added).

Thank God for Judah! Thank Him for the nation Israel! Out of His kindness, He chose Israel and made them a peculiar people. Israel, though a small nation, carried with her a unique trademark of sovereign ownership of the God of the universe. Let no one deceive you; Israel, like no other nation, has a special standing with God. That was true yesterday and is equally true today and tomorrow! In Scripture, they are called a *"holy people unto the LORD thy God"* (Deuteronomy 7:6, KJV), *"the apple of His eye"* (Zechariah 2:8), *"a people for His own possession"* (Deuteronomy 7:6), *"a kingdom of priests"* (Exodus 19:6), *"Ministers of our God"* (Isaiah 61:6, KJV), and *"like a wife"* (Isaiah 54:6). Yes, a wife! Her spousal relationship with God undoubtedly explains why God takes anti-Semitism personally (Genesis 12:3). It explains *in toto* also why God goes after any person or nation that hates Israel. Think of it! As a loving husband, would you not take it personally when someone else abuses your wife? I would; God would too—and He does! *"Blessed is everyone who blesses you, And cursed is everyone who curses you"* (Numbers 24:9). That's the Word of God!

We embrace Israel, not only for being a special people unto God, but also for being a channel whereby God revealed Himself to the human race. Simply put, they were the custodians of divine revelation (Romans 9:4-5). Whatever we know about the true God of the universe, we have come to know because of the Jewish Bible.[49] In

---

[49] The original Bible came to us from the hands of the Jews.

studying it, we come to know about God's essence. Much more, we come to discover that He is just and righteous in all His ways (Psalm 145:17). Here, then, in this chapter, it will be crystal clear to us that God, not the so-called Mother Nature or any other agent, is the supreme superintendent of every disaster in life.

A brief introduction to Israel's rise from bondage in Egypt to an era of a golden age and then back to bondage again is worthy of our attention. Israel, in 1441 B.C., was liberated from Egypt after God wrought ten powerful miracles, the last being the death of every firstborn in Egypt (Exodus 12:29-31). God, not Mother Nature or some kind of disease epidemic, was responsible for the death of every firstborn son in Egypt. Scripture alone dismisses any possible confusion as to who might be responsible: "*Now it came about at midnight that the* **LORD** *struck all the firstborn in the land of Egypt,* *from the firstborn of Pharaoh who sat on his throne to the firstborn of the captive who was in the dungeon, and all the firstborn of cattle*" (Exodus 12:29, emphasis added).

What if one morning we woke up only to hear in the news that every firstborn in our land was dead? Whom would we say is responsible? More to the point, to whom should we credit such a disaster? Read the passage one more time. "*Now it came about at midnight that the LORD struck all the firstborn in the land of Egypt.*" Scripture never shrinks from crediting disasters to the omnipotent sovereign God. We shouldn't shrink either. It doesn't make us unspiritual to say that God was responsible for 9/11 or a cyclone or any disaster for that matter! The Bible is crystal clear: "*If a trumpet is blown in a city will not the people tremble? If a calamity occurs in a city has not the LORD done it? [Is He not respon-*

sible?]" (Amos 3:6). Amos expects us to say, "Yes, the Lord is behind that earthquake" or "that devastating flood." My friend, we can never be more spiritual than Scripture itself! Consequently, when disasters occur, the question ought not to be who is responsible but rather, what kind of message is God sending us?

We have said it before. Every disciplined parent has a system of law and order in place to govern his or her household that spells out the consequences of non-compliance. The Father-God is no exception! He called out His children, Israel, and made them into a nation. Accordingly, He established a system of law and order to govern them and keep them from self-destruction. He spelled out His blessings for their obedience to His Law:

> *Now it shall be, if you diligently obey the LORD your God, being careful to do all His commandments which I command you today, the LORD your God will set you high above all the nations of the earth. All these blessings will come upon you and overtake you if you obey the LORD your God: Blessed shall you be in the city, and blessed shall you be in the country...Blessed shall be your basket and your kneading bowl* (Deuteronomy 28:1-5).

On the other hand, curses were promised for disobedience:

> *But it shall come about, if you do not obey the LORD your God, to observe to do all His commandments and His statutes with which I charge you today, that all these curses will come upon you and overtake you: Cursed shall you be in the city, and cursed shall you be in the country. Cursed shall be your basket and your*

kneading bowl [economic disaster] (Deuteronomy 28:15-17).

He reiterated:

> *See, I have set before you today life and prosperity, and death and adversity [disaster]; in that I command you today to love the LORD your God, to walk in His ways and to keep His commandments and His statutes and His judgments, that you may live and multiply, and that the LORD your God may bless you in the land where you are entering to possess it. But if your heart turns away and you will not obey, but are drawn away and worship other gods and serve them, I declare to you today that you shall surely perish. You will not prolong your days in the land where you are crossing the Jordan to enter and possess it. I call heaven and earth to witness against you today, that I have set before you life and death, the blessing and the curse. So choose life in order that you may live, you and your descendants* (Deuteronomy 30:15-19).

God has spoken! The burden of faithfulness to His Word is on His shoulders! You will agree with me that law is of no consequence if it's not implemented. God tells us in Jeremiah that He is watching over His Word to ensure its fulfillment (Jeremiah 1:12). The implication then is that God's justice must be ready to respond to His injunctions in Deuteronomy 28:1-5 and 28:15-17 respectively. In other words, His justice stands on guard to sway to any direction the Israelites choose; namely, if they choose obedience, He will bless them, and if disobedience, He will curse them.

That's true for us, for everything on Earth is His (Psalm 24:1). God is the same, yesterday, today, and forever

(Hebrews 13:8). He does not show any partiality (Romans 2:11). Whatever is good for the goose is equally good for the gander. God cannot treat us differently. In other words, He manifests His justice to the entire world with equity. Consequently, this chapter will give us much needed insight in interpreting historical trends. It will serve as a beam of light and thus will cast light on our understanding of disasters in the light of God's work. What's more, the content will leave us no room to doubt the source of all disasters, both personal and national.

With the foundation of this chapter concretely laid, we now turn to the rise and fall of Israel's golden age, the splitting of the nation, Israel's fall, Judah's barrage of warning bells, and finally its exile to Babylon.

THE RISE OF ISRAEL'S GOLDEN AGE

Our attempt is not to cover the history of Israel; that will take a separate project. But an overview is in order if we are to appreciate God's grace as far as Israel's history is concerned. We have already noted Israel's emancipation from slavery and her independence as a priest nation unto God. In addition, a careful scrutiny of Scripture reveals a rugged road of ups and downs in her history. For instance, the book of Judges in particular reflects the injunctions of Deuteronomy 28:1-5 and 28:15-17. Arguably, this book recorded a more chaotic period in Israel's history than in any other book. Again and again they rebelled against God's Law, and He responded in kind as per His injunction:

> "*I am the LORD your God, who brought you out of the land of Egypt so that you would not be their slaves, and I broke the bars of your yoke and made you walk erect.*

148

*But if you do not obey Me and do not carry out all these commandments, if, instead, you reject My statutes, and if your soul abhors My ordinances so as not to carry out all My commandments, and so break My covenant, I, in turn, will do this to you: I [God; no one else] **will appoint over you a sudden terror, consumption and fever that will waste away the eyes and cause the soul to pine away;** also, you shall sow your seed uselessly, for your enemies will eat it up. I will set My face against you so that you will be struck down before your enemies; and those who hate you will rule over you, and you will flee when no one is pursuing you"* (Leviticus 26:13-17, emphasis added).

It breaks our hearts to know that God's resolve to discipline them if they should disobey His mandates did nothing to dissuade them from their spiritual quagmire. Over and over they rebelled against God and His sovereign rule over them. In their rebellious attitude to theocratic rule, they demanded a human king instead, like other nations (1 Samuel 8:1-5). That was their last stroke of apathy toward God! This turn of event in its history displeased the prophet Samuel, as we read in Scripture:

But the thing was displeasing in the sight of Samuel when they said, "Give us a king to judge us." And Samuel prayed to the LORD. The LORD said to Samuel, "Listen to the voice of the people in regard to all that they say to you, for they have not rejected you, but they have rejected Me from being king over them. Like all the deeds which they have done since the day that I brought them up from Egypt even to this day— in that they have forsaken Me and served other gods— so they are doing to you also" (1 Samuel 8:6-8).

In view of this effect, God appointed Saul, the Benjaminite, to be the first king of Israel. Guess what? It was a disastrous experience for both Saul and his subjects. Saul was spiritually unprepared, and so were the people of Israel. He could not stir them toward God because his own steering wheel was not in God's direction. Consequently, his kingdom ended tragically.

> *So Saul died for his trespass which he committed against the LORD, because of the word of the LORD which he did not keep; and also because he asked counsel of a medium, making inquiry of it, and did not inquire of the LORD. Therefore **He** [God alone] **killed him** and turned the kingdom to David the son of Jesse* (1 Chronicles 10:13-14, cf. 1 Samuel 13:13-14, emphasis added).

The irony though, is that with Saul on the throne, the birth of monarchy in Israel's history was celebrated. However, he failed to lead the people back to God. Then David, "*a man after [God's] own heart*" (1 Samuel 13:14), a symphony of God's grace, came to the throne. He was a spiritual giant. He set the bar of obedience to God's Word beyond the reach of his contemporaries. He was a reference point to other kings who followed in his spiritual footstep.[50] He was constantly on God's radar in that the eyes of the Lord move to and fro throughout the earth, that He may strongly support those whose heart is completely His (2 Chronicles 16:9). He demonstrated obedience, and God crowned his efforts accordingly!

---

[50] Moses C. Onwubiko, *David, a Symphony of God's Grace* (forthcoming).

That's not all! He led the nation back to God and prosperity. In light of this, some scholastic observation is worth our time:

> One of Saul's basic mistakes had been his insensitivity to Israel's religious institutions, particularly the central shrine and priesthood. But David grasped the importance of Israel's spiritual heritage and sought to perpetuate and promote it. Israel could not have been truly united unless its political leader was also its religious leader. [By bringing the ark, long neglected by Saul,] to Jerusalem and [establishing it in a tent home, David] made his city the religious as well as political capital [a] master stroke [which] greatly enhanced his people's loyalty to him.[51]

"*Righteousness exalts a nation*" (Proverbs 14:34). Simply, Israel's spiritual renewal combined with David's spiritual perspicacity spiraled the nation to an unprecedented historic height, generally referred to as Israel's Golden Age. David's military conquest was unparalleled. "The most powerful kingdom in Western Asia, Israel's borders stretched from the desert to the Mediterranean, and from the Gulf of Aqaba to the outskirts of Hamath on the Orontes."[52] Unprecedented!

In David's old age, his son Solomon, who succeeded him, came into the spotlight. He was well grounded at home spiritually (1 Kings 2:1-4; 3:3). He later gave us this advice:

---

[51] William Sanford La Sor, David Allan Hubbard, Frederic William Bush, and Leslie C. Allen, *Old Testament Survey* (1982), p. 247.

[52] Ibid., p. 248.

"Train a child in the way he should go, Even when he is old he will not depart from it" (Proverbs 22:6). He came to the throne when the atmosphere was right! His father had already for forty years "forged Judah and Israel into a military entity able to dominate its neighbors." Solomon joined in and for another forty years took the nation on a path of "mercantile enterprise bringing unprecedented wealth and fame."[53] David and his son Solomon forged an unparallel monarchy that was a role model for centuries in Israel's history, but a big price was on the horizon! This brings up the issue of a crack in the nation.

ISRAEL SPLITS INTO TWO NATIONS

Solomon made a costly mistake. He married foreign women (1 Kings 11:1-3), which was contrary to God's Law (Exodus 23:31-33). This line-crossing of mixed marriage inadvertently lured him to worship other gods (1 Kings 11:5-7). His failure brought about swift and decisive action from God with lasting impact on the nation.

> *Now the LORD was angry with Solomon because his heart was turned away from the LORD, the God of Israel, who had appeared to him twice, and had commanded him concerning this thing, that he should not go after other gods; but he did not observe what the LORD had commanded. So the LORD said to Solomon, "Because you have done this, and you have not kept My covenant and My statutes, which I have commanded you, I will surely tear the kingdom from you, and will give it to your servant"* (1 Kings 11:9/11).

---

[53] Ibid., p. 244.

The Lord, of course, did fulfill His Word. Immediately after the death of Solomon, the stage was set for the split of the nation Israel (2 Chronicles 10:16-18). We do not intend to go into detail with regard to the division. But suffice it to say, the nation was divided into two, namely, Israel and Judah, Israel being the northern kingdom and Judah the southern. Prior to its division, the nation had already begun to experience spiritual maladjustment. What do we expect? Solomon, one of Israel's finest kings, had lost his spiritual bearing due to his ignorant involvement in idolatry (1 Kings 11:2-6). It was a catalyst that began a chain reaction and chaos in the nation, first with the northern kingdom, eventually spilling over to the south!

The Fall of the Northern Kingdom

Ironically, once the nation was divided into two, the northern kingdom retained the national name, Israel, under the leadership of Jeroboam, while the other kingdom was referred to as Judah. Time will not allow us a detailed discussion on the northern kingdom. Nonetheless, we shall briefly examine its attitude toward God's injunction and consequently God's response to its apathy to God's mandates.

We begin this segment of our discussion with a mind-boggling question, namely, why did Israel fail? To answer this question, we consult Scripture:

> *Now this [Israel's fall] came about, because the sons of Israel had sinned against the LORD their God, who had brought them up from the land of Egypt from under the hand of Pharaoh, king of Egypt, and they had feared [revered] other gods...The sons of Israel did things secretly which were not right against the LORD*

their God. Moreover, they built for themselves high places [for idolatry] in all their towns, from watchtower to fortified city. They set for themselves sacred pillars and Asherim on every high hill and under every green tree...They served idols, concerning which the LORD had said to them, "You shall not do this thing" (2 Kings 17:7-12).

Simply put, they had departed from God. What next can we expect? Grace comes before judgment! And so we read,

Yet the LORD warned Israel and Judah through all His prophets and every seer, saying, "Turn from your evil ways and keep My commandments, My statutes according to all the law which I commanded your fathers, and which I sent to you through My servants the prophets" (2 Kings 17:13).

But God's warning was to no avail (2 Kings 17:14-17).

As a student of the Word of God, let's assumed you lived at that time; what would your prediction be? Disaster for Israel on the horizon! You would have been correct. God raised Assyria, the most powerful nation in the world at that time (Isaiah 19:24), and in 721 B.C. used them to remove the Israelites from their land! In light of this we read,

So the LORD was very angry with Israel and removed them from His sight; none was left except the tribe of Judah...until the LORD removed Israel from His sight, as He spoke through all His servants the prophets So Israel was carried away into exile from their own land to Assyria until this day (2 Kings 17:18-23).

God keeps His Word!

Here comes an important question: If you were an Israelite who lived at the time of its exile, what would you say was the core reason for Assyria's victory over your nation? Would you say that your people were defeated because of a lack of manpower? If so, wrong! The answer is revealed in God's sovereignty: *"The Lord removed Israel from His sight!"* That's exactly what the Bible says. That means all the flaming arrows of the Assyrians and their bloody swords that cut through the nation of Israel were the handiwork of God! Again, *"If a trumpet is blown in a city will not the people tremble? If a calamity occurs in a city has not the LORD done it? [Is He not responsible?]"* (Amos 3:6). With the exile of the northern kingdom, we can now focus our attention on the southern kingdom, Judah.

THE SOUTHERN KINGDOM

To have a better appreciation for this section, we recommend that you take time and read through the book of 2 Chronicles. Twenty people sat on the throne of Judah after the death of Solomon, the first being his son Rehoboam and the last Zedekiah. The highlight of it all is that Judah outlived the northern kingdom by over a century. The northern kingdom lived for 210 years (931-721 B.C.) and Judah for 325 (931-606 B.C.).[54] What's the secret? The answer is in one word: *spiritual*! The former turned her back on God and kept on going in the direction of apostasy until there was no remedy but exile, while the latter had a series of recoveries from its spiritual quagmire and thus experienced some measure of God's grace. The truth of the matter is that God

---

[54] H. L. Willmington, *Willmington's Guide to the Bible* (Tyndale House Publishers Inc., 1984), p. 141.

never takes pleasure in the destruction of anyone; rather, He wishes that everyone should abandon their evil ways and seek Him (Ezekiel 33:11).

In the course of our study, we shall endeavor to connect the dots between obedience to God's mandates and blessing and between disobedience and disaster. Remarkably, there were less than half a dozen obedient kings in Judah's history; the rest were anything but obedient kings. The latter took the nation into a spiritual dungeon, while the former brought enlightenment, reformation, and a spark of spiritual awakening to the nation. The latter brought chaos and discomfort, while the former turned the country from chaos to quietude. Sadly, Judah too ran out of spiritual fuel and eventually was forced into exile. The warning bell is that Judah's experience can be anyone else's!

Now we are ready to examine few of the kings, both the finest and the evil ones. We begin with the first king, namely, Rehoboam.

THE REIGN OF REHOBOAM

We take on our first exercise: "*When the kingdom of Rehoboam was established and strong, he and all Israel with him forsook the law of the LORD*" (2 Chronicles 12:1). Where should the dots of they "forsook the law of the Lord" be connected? Disaster! Absolutely correct! "*And it came about in King Rehoboam's fifth year, because they had been unfaithful to the LORD, that Shishak king of Egypt came up against Jerusalem*" (v. 2). The question then is, who was behind the invasion of Judah? God, of course: "*Then Shemaiah the prophet came to Rehoboam and the princes of Judah who had gathered at Jerusalem because of Shishak, and he said to them, "Thus says the LORD, 'You have forsaken Me, so I also have forsaken you to Shishak'*" (v. 5). We see it was God who gave them over to their enemy. We are ready to take on another king.

ABIJAH

Interestingly, Jeroboam, the evil king of northern kingdom, was still in power when Abijah sat on the throne of Judah. The sharp contrast between the two was their spiritual life. Abijah was preoccupied with the Lord (2 Chronicles 13:10-12), and his counterpart was not (11:14-15). Jeroboam assumed that his military edge of 800,000 against 400,000 of Judah would earn him victory. He was wrong! He forgot King David's motto: "*The battle is the LORD's*" (1 Samuel 17:47). In the heat of the battle, his military campaign met an upper hand, God's:

> *Then the men of Judah raised a war cry, and when the men of Judah raised the war cry,* **then it was that God routed Jeroboam and all Israel before Abijah and Judah**. *When the sons of Israel fled before Judah,* **God gave them into their hand**. *Abijah and his people defeated them with a great slaughter, so that* **500,000 chosen men of Israel fell slain**. *Thus the sons of Israel were subdued at that time, and* **the sons of Judah conquered because they trusted in the LORD, the God of their fathers** (2 Chronicles 13:15-18, emphasis added).

Half a million men dead in one day! We ask, who was responsible for the death of these men? Do we hear someone murmur, "God"? That's right! *God routed Jeroboam and all Israel before Abijah and Judah!* Are we still unconvinced that God is behind every disaster, no matter how atrocious?

That's not all! *"Jeroboam did not again recover strength in the days of Abijah; and the LORD struck him and he died"* (v. 20). Today, we would try to explain away such a large number of casualties and the death of Jeroboam. My friend, time is ticking, and the immutable God is still on the throne! We need to make sure we are on His side in every sense. If we are not on His side, we need to adjust in a hurry! This brings us to yet another king, Asa.

THE REIGN OF ASA

"So Abijah slept with his fathers, and they buried him in the city of David, and his son Asa became king in his place. The land was undisturbed for ten years during his days" (2 Chronicles 14:1). Immediately we find a dot to connect: *"The land was undisturbed for ten years during his days."* Where can we connect this dot to, obedience or disobedience? Obedience, of course!

> *Asa did good and right in the sight of the LORD his God, for he removed the foreign altars and high places, tore down the sacred pillars, cut down the Asherim, and commanded Judah to seek the LORD God of their fathers and to observe the law and the commandment. He also removed the high places and the incense altars from all the cities of Judah. And the kingdom was undisturbed under him. He built fortified cities in Judah, since the land was undisturbed, and there was no one at war with him during those years, because the LORD had given him rest* (2 Chronicles 14:2-6).

The Lord kept his enemies at bay for ten years! On the other hand, at the end of those years, the Lord permitted the powerful Ethiopian army to challenge Asa. Recall that we had already delineated that not all disasters are related to spiritual failures. Here's a perfect example. *"Now Zerah the Ethiopian came out against them with an army of a million men and 300 chariots, and he came to Mareshah"* (2 Chronicles 14:9). Asa was outnumbered by a ratio of 2:1, for he had only an army of 580,000 men (2 Chronicles 14:8). Often God allows suffering or disaster to hit those who are obedient to His Word so that He might demonstrate His sufficiency in all things. Guess what Asa did at this crossroads. He turned to his God in prayer. Absolutely! But not so fast! This prepares us to briefly examine prayer in conjunction with our study.

INSTANT PRAYER IN A DARK TIME

Prayer is a powerful weapon when used in accordance with God's will. We often think that prayer is like a switch we can flip back and forth when we are in a dark room of life or in a jam. We are probably right. But it functions under divine principles. Like electrical light, all its wiring must be properly connected; otherwise, light will not come on when the switch is turned on. Similarly, the electrical prayer line must be in order! There are no two ways about it!

As a student of the Word of God, doesn't it make you nauseated to hear such thing as national prayer by a nation whose lifeline is disconnected from the powerhouse of Heaven? The truth is that national prayer that's devoid of reverence to God is nothing but a mockery. Simply, a nation that disregards the Word of God is a nation that angers God with its prayer. *"[A nation or] he who turns away his ear from listening to the law, Even his prayer is an abomination [to God]"* (Proverbs 28:9). *"So when you spread out your hands in prayer, I will hide My eyes from you; Yes, even though you mul-*

159

tiply prayers, I will not listen. Your hands are covered with blood" (Isaiah 1:15).

Prayer is conditional (2 Chronicles 7:14). Obedience to God's Word is the electrical wire that connects our light bulb to the powerhouse in Heaven (1 John 3:22; John 15:7). God's promise in Psalm 50:15, which states, "*Call upon Me in the day of trouble; I shall rescue you, and you will honor Me,*" is for the obedient children of God (Psalm 34:17). It doesn't work for those who are disobedient to His Word (50:16). That's why many prayers go unanswered. Asa knew all that, and so he turned his prayer switch on, because his spiritual life was distinctly wired:

> *So Asa went out to meet him, and they drew up in battle formation in the valley of Zephathah at Mareshah. Then Asa called to the LORD his God, and said, "There is no one besides You to help in the battle between the powerful and those who have no strength; so help us, O LORD our God, for we trust in You, and in Your name have come against this multitude. O LORD, You are our God; let not man prevail against You"* (2 Chronicles 14:10,11).

What a prayer from a soul saturated with God's Word!

God is always faithful; consequently, in response to His Word (Psalm 50:15),

> *The LORD routed the Ethiopians before Asa and before Judah, and the Ethiopians fled. Asa and the people who were with him pursued them as far as Gerar; and so many Ethiopians fell that they could not recover, for they were shattered before the LORD and before His army. And they carried away very much plunder* (2 Chronicles 14:12-13).

Again, any illusion as to who handed the Ethiopians untold number of casualties? *"The LORD routed the Ethiopians before Asa...for they were shattered before the LORD and before His army."*

We will consider yet another spiritual giant.

JEHOSHAPHAT

Jehoshaphat was one of the finest kings in Judah's history and was instrumental in its spiritual awakening during its turbulent time. The truth is that there can be no tranquility in a nation until the souls of its citizens are tranquilized with the Word of God!

Realizing that God's Word is the lifeline of any people, Jehoshaphat emphasized the teaching of the Law. He employed Bible teachers and sent them to the people: *"They taught in Judah, having the book of the law of the LORD with them; and they went throughout all the cities of Judah and taught among the people"* (2 Chronicles 17:9). The result? Profound!

We are not finished with our dot connecting. *"The Lord was with Jehoshaphat because..."* Connect the dot. He was with him because of his obedience to God's Word.

> *The LORD was with Jehoshaphat because he followed the example of his father David's earlier days and did not seek the Baals, but sought the God of his father, followed His commandments, and did not act as Israel did. So the LORD established the kingdom in his control, and all Judah brought tribute to Jehoshaphat, and he had great riches and honor* (2 Chronicles 17:3-5).

On the other hand, God in His sovereignty permitted his neighboring countries to join in alliance against Jehoshaphat.

161

Militarily, he was outnumbered in every sense of the word! What did he do? He turned to the Lord in prayer (2 Chronicles 20:3-12). God has told us that those who trust in Him will never be put to shame (Isaiah 28:16). In light of what we have studied so far, do we think that he would be shamed? Not at all! Not if we believe the Word of God!

The Lord told him not to fear, for He would fight the battle for him (2 Chronicles 20:15). What did the Lord do? He caused great confusion among the enemies of Jehoshaphat, and they fought one another until there were corpses everywhere (2 Chronicles 20:20-24). That's right; they ambushed themselves.

How quick we are in explaining away incidents. I believe if such a thing were to happen in our day, we would some way, somehow, explain it away. We might say that the victorious troops sneaked some kind of mind-altering drugs into their enemies' drinking water or something like that. Were we not quick in explaining away 9/11? What about the tsunami? Hurricane Katrina? Didn't we explain them away as effects of the so-called global warming? The list can go on and on! Tragically, God is never in the equation of our rationalization! Nevertheless, because of the spiritual integrity of Judah under the spiritual leadership of Jehoshaphat, God gave them peace all around. And so we read, "*And the dread of God was on all the kingdoms of the lands when they heard that the LORD had fought against the enemies of Israel. So the kingdom of Jehoshaphat was at peace, for his God gave him rest on all sides*" (2 Chronicles 20:29-30).

It's of paramount importance that we pause and consider the dots we have connected so far in light of our definition of God's sovereignty. Recall that we defined sovereignty to mean that the Creator-God has absolute, supreme, airtight control in everything as He directs and that He superintends all events of the universe in accordance with the counsel of His will (Ephesians 1:11). Indeed, God is in charge! Always! We saw in our connections the correlations between obedience and blessings and disobedience and disasters respectively. My question then is, why are we too scared to credit God for unusual outbursts of floods, earthquakes, terrorism, and the like as punishments for our disobedience to His Word?

This brings us to the next king.

Jehoram

"*Jehoram was thirty-two years old when he became king, and he reigned eight years in Jerusalem. He walked in the way of the kings of Israel, just as the house of Ahab did (for Ahab's daughter was his wife), and he did evil in the sight of the LORD*" (2 Chronicles 21:5-6). We see our first connecting point: "*He did evil in the sight of the LORD.*" Where is our next connecting point? Disaster! We are right again!

> ***Then the LORD stirred up against Jehoram the spirit of the Philistines and the Arabs*** *who bordered the Ethiopians; and they came against Judah and invaded it, and carried away all the possessions found in the king's house together with his sons and his wives, so that no son was left to him except Jehoahaz, the youngest of his sons. So **after all this the LORD smote him in his bowels with an incurable sickness**. Now it came about in the course of time, at the end of two years, that his bowels came out because of his sickness and he died in great pain. And his people made no fire for him like the fire for his fathers*" (2 Chronicles 21:16-19, emphasis added).

Here again we see God's sovereignty in operation. First, He stirred up the spirit of Philistines and Arabs, and they invaded Judah and made their lives miserable. That's a warning bell from the supreme court of Heaven. Considering this, for instance, would we be remiss to say that God stirred up the spirit of the 9/11 terrorists? Think of it! Second, "*the LORD smote [the king] in his bowels with an incurable sickness.*" Then on the third strike, the Lord took him out: "*Now it came about in the course of time, at the end of two years, that his bowels came out because of his sickness and he died in great pain.*" My friend, the same God of Jehoram reigns supreme, and His justice is unchanging! Consequently, all disasters in life are coded with a message, and so let us be experts in decoding them. In times of calamity, let's reflect!

After the death of Joash, the youngest king in Judah's history (seven years old), the nation spun onto a spiritual roller coaster. The land went into spiritual darkness. God sent them warning bells through military defeats. Consequently, Hezekiah took the throne and brought the nation back to God.

HEZEKIAH, THE LAST REFORMER

We can never emphasize this enough: blessed is any man or nation that submits to the sovereign rule of God (Psalm 33:12). Hezekiah understood concretely the justice of God. He knew the blessing of obedience and consequences of the reverse. Consequently, like his grandfather David, he took the route of obedience to God (2 Chronicles 29:2). That's not all; he ignited a spiritual reformation in the nation.

CAMPAIGN FOR SPIRITUAL REFORMATION

When there is chaos in a nation, priests are the ones to be indicted first (Malachi 1:6). Hosea, the last prophet who sounded a warning bell to the northern kingdom before they were deported to Assyria, illustrated this concept beautifully (Hosea 4:1-10). God sent Israel a series of warning bells, but all to no avail. Israel failed *"Because they [had] stopped giving heed to the LORD"* (Hosea 4:10). Jehoshaphat knew all this and wanted to implement reformation in order to avert God's wrath. He challenged the people to turn back to the Lord. And so we read,

> *Then he said to them, "Listen to me, O Levites [servants of the Most High]. Consecrate yourselves now, and consecrate the house of the LORD, the God of your fathers, and carry the uncleanness out from the holy place. For our fathers have been unfaithful and have done evil in the sight of the LORD our God, and have forsaken Him and turned their faces away from the dwelling place of the LORD, and have turned their backs. They have also shut the doors of the porch and put out the lamps, and have not burned incense or offered burnt offerings in the holy place to the God of Israel"* (2 Chronicles 29:5-7).

Let's pause for a moment and connect the dots. Right away we see the first point of connection: *"For our fathers have been unfaithful and have done evil in the sight of the LORD our God, and have forsaken Him and turned their faces away from [Him]."* Question: where do we think our next connecting point will lead to? Definitely it will take us to disaster!

The king went on to make a connection between their present spiritual condition and their national suffering:

> *"Therefore the wrath of the LORD was against Judah and Jerusalem, and **He has made them an object of terror, of horror, and of hissing, as you see with your own eyes.** For behold, our fathers have fallen by the sword, and our sons and our daughters and our wives are in captivity for this"* (2 Chronicles 29:8-9, emphasis added).

He then offered them the solution: *"Now it is in my heart to make a covenant with the LORD God of Israel, that His burning anger may turn away from us"* (2 Chronicles 29:10). *"And [if] My people who are called by My name [should] humble themselves and pray and seek My face and turn from their wicked ways, then I will hear from heaven, will forgive their sin and will heal their land"* (2 Chronicles 7:14).

The priests did accordingly (2 Chronicles 29:12-19), and Hezekiah restored temple worship (2 Chronicles 29:20-30:1-9) and reinstituted Passover (2 Chronicles 30:13-27), which had been abandoned for a long period of time because of the nation's spiritual quagmire. *"Thus Hezekiah did throughout all Judah; and he did what was good, right, and true before the LORD his God. Every work which he began in the service of the house of God in law and in commandment, seeking his God, he did with all his heart and prospered"* (2 Chronicles 31:20-21).

He prospered; or better, the Lord prospered him because his spiritual life was in order! My friend, we cannot experience true prosperity until our spiritual lives register positively on the scale of Heaven. It's comforting to know that the Lord is with you when you are with Him. And if you seek

Him, He will let you find Him; but if you forsake Him, He will forsake you (not as His child; rather He will give you over to severe discipline).

As for Hezekiah, he had taken the nation back to the Lord. Guess what? He would soon be ambushed by the world's most powerful nation, Assyria. But guess what again? God would use the occasion to demonstrate the difference between obedience and disobedience, as we have seen time and time again in our study. To this effect we read, *"After these acts of faithfulness [to the Lord] Sennacherib king of Assyria came and invaded Judah and besieged the fortified cities, and thought to break into them for himself"* (2 Chronicles 32:1). Hezekiah called on his God for help (2 Chronicles 32:20), and He responded. God stopped the war even before it began: *"Then it happened that night that the angel of the LORD went out and struck 185,000 in the camp of the Assyrians; and when men rose early in the morning, behold, all of them were dead"* (2 Kings 19:35). That's 185,000 struck dead in one night! Who struck them dead? The Lord of the armies! He sent the most powerful king home totally devastated and totally defeated! If this passage doesn't get our attention about the fact that the Lord is the Lord of history, we don't know which other passage of Scripture will do that for us. Disaster is God's monopoly! *"If a trumpet is blown in a city will not the people tremble? If a calamity occurs in a city has not the LORD done it? [Is He not responsible?]"* (Amos 3:6).

This prepares us to take a close look at King Zedekiah, the last straw on the throne of Judah before its Babylonian captivity.

ZEDEKIAH, THE LAST STRAW

Sooner or later, those who are apathetic and indifferent to God's Word will draw their last grace check from the bank of grace! Judah was a perfect example of those who went through a barrage of warning disciplines, all to no avail. Zedekiah, an evil king (2 Chronicles 36:12), was the last straw. God had exhausted His earmarked grace account for Judah. And so we read,

> *The LORD, the God of their fathers, sent word to them again and again by His messengers, because He had compassion on His people and on His dwelling place; but they continually mocked the messengers of God, despised His words and scoffed at His prophets, until the wrath of the LORD arose against His people, until there was no remedy* (2 Chronicles 36:15-16).

Think of it: God prepared Jeremiah, the last prophet (just as this book may be your last prophet), who preached relentlessly for twenty-three years to warn them. Jeremiah himself tells us,

> *"From the thirteenth year of Josiah the son of Amon, king of Judah, even to this day, these twenty-three years the word of the LORD has come to me, and I have spoken to you again and again, but you have not listened. And the LORD has sent to you all His servants the prophets again and again, but you have not listened nor inclined your ear to hear, saying, 'Turn now everyone from his evil way and from the evil of your deeds, and dwell on the land which the LORD has given to you and your forefathers forever and ever; and do not go after other gods to serve them and to worship*

them, and do not provoke Me to anger with the work of your hands, and I will do you no harm.' Yet you have not listened to Me," declares the LORD, "in order that you might provoke Me to anger with the work of your hands to your own harm" (Jeremiah 25:3-7).

Yes, they had reached the point of no return! This could happen to anyone, or any nation for that matter. My beloved, we ought to cease and desist from explaining away unusual floods, all-out hurricanes, tornadoes, or even recessions. These are God's messengers (Psalm 104:4). We ought not to keep on buying time as did Judah until their last check was used up! The Lord is warning us! Will we heed His voice? *"For He says, 'at the acceptable time I listened to you, and on the day of salvation I helped you.' Behold, now is 'the acceptable time,' behold, now is 'the day of salvation'"* (2 Corinthians 6:2).

THE FALL OF JUDAH

We need to pay close attention to the fall of Judah, the southern kingdom. Watch out for the hand of God in its fall: *"Therefore He [God] brought up against them the king of the Chaldeans who slew their young men with the sword in the house of their sanctuary, and had no compassion on young man or virgin, old man or infirm;* **He gave them all into his hand"** (2 Chronicles 36:17, emphasis added). Jeremiah, the last prophet to Judah, tells us in his own words,

> *"Therefore thus says the LORD of hosts, 'Because you have not obeyed My words, behold, I will send and take all the families of the north,' declares the LORD, 'and I will send to Nebuchadnezzar king of Babylon, My servant, and will bring them against this land and*

169

against its inhabitants and against all these nations round about; and I will utterly destroy them and make them a horror and a hissing, and an everlasting desolation. Moreover, I will take from them the voice of joy and the voice of gladness, the voice of the bridegroom and the voice of the bride, the sound of the millstones and the light of the lamp. This whole land will be a desolation and a horror, and these nations will serve the king of Babylon seventy years" (Jeremiah 25:8-11).

Imagine living in Iraq during Saddam Hussein's regime and hearing a minister call him God's servant! That's exactly what Jeremiah did—He called Nebuchadnezzar, a ruthless, heartless, and dubious king, God's servant. Scripture tells us that all things are God's servants (Psalm 119:91). This means that every vessel is at His disposal! My friend, that's what sovereignty is all about! Judah went into exile because of its attitude toward God's injunction. No nation is indispensable! We are forced to conclude that any nation that follows in the footsteps of Judah is likely to suffer a similar fate, but in varying degrees, since no nation is alike. Judah is out of our discussion for the moment, making way for an in-depth examination of what's happening in America.

10 | God's Warning Bell in America

"I tremble for my country when I reflect that God is just; and His justice cannot sleep for ever" (Thomas Jefferson).

Will America Outlive Rome? This book is a work in progress, so we will not cover as much ground here as we intend to do in that book concerning the state of America. Suffice it to say, there's much parallelism between the empire of Rome and America. Equally comparable is the symmetrical resemblance between America and Judah, the southern kingdom of Israel. No doubt about it; only a handful of historians, if any at all, would argue the fact that Christianity impacted the world of the Roman Empire. The impact reverberated throughout the empire and swirled into other European countries, such as Great Britain, as we previously delineated.

We just concluded looking at the impact of the obedience and disobedience of Mosaic Law on both the northern and southern kingdoms of Israel. We noted the indelible mark of true Judaism on the society of Israel and how their abuse of it brought disaster on their nation. We now ask, what about America?

Russell Kirk puts it: "Both the direct influence and the indirect influence of religion [Christianity] upon American society were incalculable strong."[55] C. Gregg Singer said: "A Christian world and life view furnished the basis for this early political thought which guided the American people for nearly two centuries and whose crowning lay in the writing of the Constitution of 1787."[56] Its unparalleled blessing is revealed in Scripture: "*When a man's ways are pleasing to the LORD, He [God] makes even his enemies to be at peace with him*" (Proverbs 16:7; cf. 2 Chronicles 14:2-6;15:15;17:3-10).

Singer wrote,

> Whether we look at the Puritans and their fellow colonists of the seventeenth century, or their descendants of the eighteenth century, or those who framed the Declaration of Independence and the Constitution, we see that their political programs were the rather clear reflection of a consciously held political philosophy, and that the various political philosophies which emerged among the American people were intimately related to the theological developments which were taking place.[57]

In view of this, we read afresh the words of McGuffey (1800-1873), the schoolmaster of the United States of America: "The Christian religion is the religion of our

---

[55] Russell Kirk, *The Roots of American Order* (Washington, DC: Regnery Gateway, 1991), p. 332.

[56] C. Gregg Singer, *A Theological Interpretation of American History* (Greenville, SC: A Press, 1994), pp. 325-326.

[57] Ibid., p. 333.

country. From it are derived our prevalent notions of the character of God, the great moral governor of the universe. On its doctrines are founded the peculiarities of our free institutions." Larry Schweikart, a professor of history at University of Dayton, wrote,

> Religious revivals washed over America in six great waves, ranging from the Puritan migration and Great Awakening of the seventeenth and eighteenth centuries...Throughout the 1815-1860 period, religious enthusiasm characterized American culture, from the churches of New England, to the camp meetings on western frontiers, to the black slave churches of the Old South.[58]

In addition, he said, "hundreds of thousands of Americans found answers to their profound spiritual questions in Protestant Christianity."[59] My question is, who can argue these things?

In light of the commonality among the three nations, Judah, Rome, and America, in the God of the universe, we wish to examine the effect of desertion of these two nations from God and what that means for America. First, let's briefly discuss the Roman Empire.

ROMAN EMPIRE AT LARGE

It is said that "any particular society that has departed from the great body of the nation, or religion to which it belonged, immediately becomes the object of universal as

---

[58] Larry Schweikart and Michael Allen, *A Patriot's History of the United States* (New York: Penguin Group, 2004), p. 221.

[59] Ibid., p. 221.

well as invidious (unenviable) observation."[60] As the happiness of a future life is the great object of religion, we may hear without surprise or scandal that the introduction, or at least the abuse of Christianity, had some influence on the decline and fall of the Roman Empire.[61]

Edward Gibbon (1737-1794) in his *Decline and the Fall of the Roman Empire* (1776-1788) said that the following five attributes marked Rome at its end: first, a mounting love of show of luxury (that is, affluence); second, a widening gap between the very rich and the very poor (this could be among countries in the family of nations as well as in a single nation); third, an obsession with sex; fourth, freakishness in the arts, masquerading as originality, and enthusiasms pretending to be creativity; and fifth, an increased desire to live off the state. It all sounds so familiar. We have come a long road...and we are back in Rome.[62]

Simply stated, Rome suffered internal injury when Christianity lost its grip on its purpose, mission, and impact on the people of the Roman Empire, and from that point on, Rome spiraled downward until it was no more. This takes us back to revisit the episode of the southern kingdom, Judah.

JUDAH REVISITED

We have already discussed in detail the fall of Judah; however, we consider it of paramount importance to revisit a portion of this section in order to help us see the pattern of God's justice. We have also seen a close similarity between Rome and Judah. We may want to reread chapter 9 before

---

[60] Gibbon, *The Decline and Fall of the Roman Empire*, p. 164.

[61] Ibid., p. 525.

[62] Schaeffer, *How Should We Then Live?* p. 227.

continuing in order to reacquaint ourselves with what happened in Judah. We saw how God prepared Nebuchadnezzar and used him as an instrument of punishment on Judah because of its disobedience of the principles of Judaism. God sent them warnings again and again until there was no recourse, until His justice prevailed (2 Chronicles 36:15).

As a result, they were taken to exile in 606 B.C. because of their colossal spiritual failure. It boils down to this: if two out of three nations that shared spiritual bonds as earlier stated suffered tragically because of their attitude toward God, it would make sense to conclude that the third nation—the United States—will suffer too if it turns away from God. Maybe we have somewhat departed and thus are already paying the piper.

BREAKDOWN OF CHRISTIANITY IN AMERICA

For many days Israel was without the true God and without a teaching priest and without law. But in their distress they turned to the LORD God of Israel, and they sought Him, and He let them find Him. In those times there was no peace to him who went out or to him who came in, for many disturbances afflicted all the inhabitants of the lands (2 Chronicles 15:3-5).

We see that the first indictment was on the priests. We can never say it enough: a breakdown in a society starts with gross negligence of the accurate communication of Scripture or a total abandonment of divine establishment all together. We see this from coast-to-coast, people mishandling Scriptural truth (2 Timothy 4:3-4). The effect of the accurate dissemination of God's Word cannot be measured!

Russell Kirk quotes Rowland Berthoff in his groundbreaking study of order and disorder in American social history: "The history of American society strongly suggests that if men subvert or abandon the values embodied in a well-ordained institutional structure, and so dismantle the social foundations for cultural achievement and spiritual serenity, they proceed at their own grave peril."[63]

America had frequently experienced spiritual coldness and subsequently bounced back to God, a period known as the Great Awakening or revival times. That was equally true of Rome and Judah. We saw in the last chapter that Judah regained spiritual momentum under the electrifying spiritual flame of kings like Jehoshaphat, Hezekiah, and a handful of others. But hold it! They also went to the point of no return and eventually lost God's glory in their respective kingdoms! Hence we should never have the attitude of "Let's live it up; we will bounce back as we always do." Rather, our attitude ought to be that of a humble mind and a change of mental attitude toward the God of the universe with the hope that we are not on our way out, as were others.

We ask, "In what ways have we lost our grip on Christianity?" Judah asked similar question in Malachi 3:7 when their land was in disarray. It's not the purpose of this book to dissect the spiritual failures in America. There's a saying that you do not need a mirror to examine your wristwatch. Accordingly, anyone can write an essay on just about any topic from a countless list of spiritual degeneracy in America. Nevertheless, we need to draw our attention to just a few of our spiritual relapses and the decisive response of the supreme court of Heaven. But before we do, let's reconsider God's justice.

---

[63] Kirk, *The Roots of American Order*, p. 442.

THE JUSTICE OF GOD REVISITED

We have said it before: we are people of sentiments. We get excited when we hear the word _love_. God is not sentimental! Emotion wanes and waxes. God's unchanging character (Malachi 3:6) keeps Him in check from experiencing the mood swings of love like we do. God is love and equally a God of justice. He cannot compromise His Holiness on account of love. There's always a balance between the two. We have witnessed the expression of His love and justice on both the northern and southern kingdoms of Israel. With that in our minds, it makes no sense for us to see or hear of a disaster and ask, "How could a loving God do such a horrible thing to people?" The right question would be, "How could a just God not do more to a people who have no respect for Him?" With that said, we begin with the breakdown of marriage in America.

MARRIAGE BREAKDOWN

We have previously examined the condition of marriage in the United States of America. Tom Elliff correctly made the assertion that "America has become saturated in a 'divorce culture.'"[64] Researchers found, namely, that more than 50 percent of all marriages in the America end up in divorce.[65] It was broken down on a daily average, which amounts to about 3,571 divorces! That's 3,571 shattered homes in America every day, prompting Elliff's further statement: "Any breakup of a marriage is a funeral of a home, which is something more Christians need to take seriously."

---

[64] Baptist Press, 2005.

[65] Jennifer Baker, Forest Institute of Professional Psychology in Springfield, Missouri.

He added, "It's one thing to grieve over 3,000 people who died in the World Trade Center, and I did over that, but if that day was like every other day in America, more than that many homes died."[66] We reiterate: who can argue that a disaster in marriage is a disaster in the chemistry of the rearing up of children? How our children have fallen on the wayside of shattered homes!

God no longer speaks to us today as He did in time past.[67] We need to reflect on a passage of Scripture and then make a connection to our time. "*If there is a man who lies with a male as those who lie with a woman, both of them have committed a detestable act; they shall surely be put to death. Their bloodguiltiness is upon them*" (Leviticus 20:13). You read it correctly! God calls such behavior detestable, an act punishable by death. The irony is that God calls it an abominable act but America in its present state calls it sexual orientation. With such a contrast between our view and God's, we connect the next dots under the beam of light of His justice. The passing of the Proposition 8 in California on Nov. 5, 2008, which barred same-sex marriage, is a signal of a blinking light of hope in America. But what ahppened before then was really disturbing in light of the justice of God. On May 15, 2008, the California Supreme Court ruled that excluding same-sex couples from marriage is unconstitutional, effectively creating same-sex marriage in California. Right away we find a point of connection, namely, legalization of same-sex marriage in defiance of God's moral law. This is simply a begging for divine

---

[66] Baptist Press, 2005.

[67] Moses C. Onwubiko, *Signs and Wonders* (2007).

judgment! It's an attack on divine institution of marriage. It's an attempt to erode God's Word and eventually destroy the divine establishment of marriage. That's satanic! God takes such an attack on His Word seriously and swiftly responds in kind through the warning bells of disasters such as terrorism and economic depression. When we brush God's Word aside, sooner or later He will hit us where it hurts most!

GOD'S WARNING BELL VIA TERRORISM

But if you do not obey Me and do not carry out all these commandments, if, instead, you reject My statutes, and if your soul abhors My ordinances so as not to carry out all My commandments, and so break My covenant, I [God, the Sovereign One, who controls history], in turn, will do this to you [Israel, Europe, USA or any nation for that matter]: I will appoint over you a ***sudden terror, consumption and fever that shall waste away the eyes and cause the soul to pine away;*** *also, you shall sow your seed uselessly, for your enemies shall eat it up. I will set My face against you so that you will be struck down before your enemies; and those who hate you will rule over you, and* ***you will flee when no one is pursuing you*** (Leviticus 26:14-17, emphasis added).

We ask, according to the Holy Scripture, who is responsible for sending terrorists on a mission? God or Al-Qaeda? Of course God, for the Psalmist said succinctly that all things are God's servants (Psalm 119:91). Nevertheless, does the above passage (Leviticus) ring a bell?

What about 9/11? The liberals, both theologians and secular, did a profound job in explaining the event of 9/11 away. They invoked every means to aid them but the Bible.

They argued, how can a loving God allow such heartless people to do such a thing to His creatures? But what does the Bible say?

God specifically said that if we disregard His Word, one way He will get our attention will be to send us a sudden terror. The passage is worth reading afresh: "*I [God, not the Islamic militants] will appoint over you a **sudden terror, consumption and fever that shall waste away the eyes and cause the soul to pine away**.*" As a sovereign God, He is entitled to use any means, such as hurricanes (Psalm 104:4), military power (2 Chronicles 36:15) and even terrorism (Leviticus 26:16), to name just a few of His messengers, to send a strong message of dissatisfaction to any nation that disregards His Word! We read the words of George Washington anew: "The propitious smiles of Heaven can never be expected on a nation that disregards the eternal rules of order and right which Heaven itself [God] has ordained."

My friend, since 9/11, America has remained in a state of *"consumption and fever"* that continually wastes away her eyes and causes her soul to pine away. Think of the constant fear that generates from Homeland Security with their color-coded security level alerts: green, blue, yellow, orange, and red. Well, the Bible tells us that it's a terrifying thing for man to fall into the hands of the Living God (Hebrews 10:31).

When we carefully scrutinize Scripture, it appears that the United States of America is facing similar divine discipline as did Judah, Rome and Great Britain! The parallels between our present experience and the record of Scripture are clear (Leviticus 26:14-17). Recall that immediately after the 9/11 incident people flooded stores across the nation, buying duct tape and sealing off their doors and windows in fear of a gas attack. Let us read the last paragraph afresh: *"You will flee when no one is pursuing you*" (Leviticus 26:17). There weren't any gas attack on the horizon! We were already fleeing. God keeps His Word!

We ask, "What's the purpose of God's warning bells?" The answer, in four words: to get our attention! "*If also after these things [warning bells] you do not obey Me, then I will punish you seven times more for your sins*" (Leviticus 26:18). We have experienced the warning bells of terrorism, and they only got our attention for a few weeks or so. That didn't help. Consequently, God is sending us another warning bell.

ECONOMIC DISASTER

Both the Roman Empire and Judah experienced economic woes when God was no longer central in their affairs. America has begun to share their fate. My friend, we should never forget that God has a monopoly both in blessings and curses. Housing markets and financial institutions cannot collapse apart from God's endorsement. That's sovereignty! Isaiah tells us that God is the One who forms light and creates darkness, the One who causes well-being and creates calamity; that He is the Lord who does all these (Isaiah 45:7).

> "*Son of man, if a country sins against Me by committing unfaithfulness, and I stretch out My hand against it, destroy its supply of bread [economic woes], send famine against it, and cut off from it both man and beast, even though these three men, Noah, Daniel, and Job [believers of spiritual integrity] were in its midst, by their own righteousness they could only deliver themselves,*" declares the Lord GOD* (Ezekiel 14:13-14).

We ask, does the above passage ring a bell? When was the last time you went to a grocery store? The truth of the matter is that any student of God's Word will not have a hard time tracing our present turbulent times back to Scripture. God has spoken! We can take any market slump and demonstrate how it can choke our economy in a hurry. Take, for instance, the gas market. At $10.00 a gallon, it can put major airlines out of business for good. What will that do to other sectors? Obviously, it will send a shock wave across every market square in the nation. Besides, it will drain your bank account in a hurry! It's beyond the scope of this book to analyze the effect of the high cost of gasoline in our economy. But suffice it to say, my beloved, we can play monkey games with our neighbors; that we cannot do with the Sovereign God of the universe!

The irony is that many of us are not seeing the finger of God in all this. We have economists telling us that next year will be worse than this year, and then we will rebound. That sounds familiar. It's nothing but political rhetoric! Of course, if you are a student of history or the Bible, it will all sound alike. That was true in the time of Rome and equally true in the time of Judah. God sent warning bells to them, but false prophets (comparable to our economists) were going around deceiving them with false message. Jeremiah, the last prophet that sounded a message of warning bells to Judah, tells us: "*They [people of falsehood] have healed the brokenness of My people superficially, Saying, 'Peace, peace,' But there is no peace*" (Jeremiah 6:14). I ask, are we being consoled superficially by the economists who keep promising us an economic rebound by the next quarter? My friend, we are heading for trouble unless there's a change of mind toward God!

We are now ready to take up one more fragment of breakdown in Christianity in our nation.

ABOLITION OF BIBLES AND RELATED MATTERS IN PUBLIC SCHOOLS

Consider this: The first chairman of the American Bible Society was Thomas Jefferson. In 1782, the United States Congress voted this resolution: "The Congress of the United States recommends and approves the Holy Bible for use in all schools." Time has really changed, and time will not give us the luxury to dissect the increasing threat of the epidemic of liberalism in America. It has done more harm than good. C. Gregg Singer pointed out in his book *A Theological Interpretation of American History* that the recently successful efforts to remove the Bible and all Christian activity from the public schools must be understood in the light of alliance between theological and political democracy.[68]

Who is the nation's schoolmaster today? It used to be William Homes McGuffey (1800-1873), but I guess Europe is our newest self-appointed schoolmaster! The truth is that one cannot give what one does not have. Europe cannot give us spiritual light, because its own light had been extinguished.

A fierce controversy over any mention of Europe's Christian heritage erupted in 2004 when officials were drafting a constitution for the European Union...Any mention of the continent's religious past or contributions of Christian culture—in a preface citing the sources of Europe's distinct civilization—would be exclusionary and offensive to non-Christians, many argued. Former French president Valery Giscard d'Estaing, who presided over the

---

[68] Singer, *A Theological Interpretation of American History*, p. 333.

process, summed up the dominant view: "Europeans live in a purely secular political system, where religion does not play an important role."[69]

That's right; Christianity has no value in modern-day European society, and her aim is to make sure America joins in, in their world of postmodernism! Europe is a spiritually dried-up land, and we seem to be heading that way.

In his 2001 book, *The Death of the West,* conservative commentator Patrick Buchanan argues that a European-style "de-Christianization of America" is the goal of many liberals—and they are succeeding. Court decisions that have banned school-sponsored prayer, removed many Nativity scenes from public squares, and legalized gay marriage are part of that pattern, as is the legal effort to erase "In God We Trust" from U.S. currency and "under God" from the Pledge of Allegiance. Europe is showing us where this path leads. It is not the right path for America.[70]

The fact is that righteousness exalts a nation, and sin is a disgrace to any people (Proverbs 14:34). Spiritual integrity subdues evil, and the reverse opens a window of opportunity for evil to soar high like a kite! Tony Blankley, in his book, *The West's Last Chance,* sounded an alarm of the threat of the Islamic extremism, but the *real* threat to the West, particularly America, is a loss of *spiritual bearing.* He said,

---

[69] Gannon, "Is God dead in Europe?"

[70] Ibid.

For centuries, the Christian faith and its embodiment in the Church formed, shaped, inspired, and governed Europe. But now the question on many minds is whether Europe will no longer be a Christian continent, but a predominantly Muslim launching pad for terrorist assaults on as a still proudly Judeo-Christian America.[71]

We need to do one thing, and one thing alone: return to God in a hurry—that's to say, if we have any aspirations of a glorious country for us today and for our children and great-grandchildren in the years to come! We reiterate: there's no smoke without a fire. There's no benefit to explaining disasters in our nation or lives away.

We are now ready to examine one of the pivotal ideas of this book, reflection.

---

[71] Tony Blankley, *The West's Last Chance: Will We Win the Clash of Civilization?* (Washington, DC: Regnery Publishing Inc., 2005), p. 152.

11 | Gateway to Reflection

Before I was afflicted I went astray, But now I keep Your word...It is good for me that I was afflicted, That I may learn Your statutes (Psalm 119:67-71).

As we come to the end of our work, we are reminded that we live in a sin-fragmented world, a world of great turmoil, frequent turbulence, and endless instability. Of course, all this was brought about when God's perfection in creation was lost in the Garden through Adam's disobedience (Genesis 2:16-17). The truth of the matter is that what we see around us today, the bad, the ugly, and the evil, are all the by-products of the fall (Genesis 3:1-7). We cannot get around it. God's perfection was stained, and consequently everything therein was thrown into chaos.

The fall brought about genetic mutations and various diseases in our world. The experience of chronic aches and pains in our bodies as old age closes in is part of the package that comes from the fall. As we approach irreversible age syndrome, our entire nervous system breaks down. Our immune system begins to shut down; it begins to lose its grip on its defensive mechanism of protection against foreign invasion of diseases. These are unavoidable facts of life!

That's not all! As long as we are in this body, we shall continue to suffer minor health issues, like flu, headaches, or stomach upsets and the like.

By now, it will have become apparent to you that minor illnesses, such as headache, are not within our study. But terminal illness and major disaster are in focus. Recall we have already noted that not all disasters are as a result of discipline and so not all terminal illnesses are as a result of sin. Repeat: we ought to cease and desist from the habit of explaining disasters away. We ought to be a people of prudence who are masters in deciphering disasters. We ought to be people of reflection! There is hope in the midst of dilemma.

REFLECTION DEFINED

Reflection is an act of soul retreat whereby one intensively searches one's soul and retraces one's ways of life and past actions in light of cause and effect. It goes without saying that *there is no smoke without a fire;* similarly, there is a purpose in everything God does. We are acutely aware of the fact that God, in His sovereign will and purpose, controls every event of human history in accordance with His eternal counsel, as noted previously. There are no accidents, bad luck, or good luck in His plan. Instead, there's a divine message in every dilemma in life.

Generally, God sends a message to us through disaster. This message is directed to three groups of people, namely, the unsaved, the carnal, and spiritually minded believers. First, God in His infinite grace and mercy—who never desires that anyone should perish but rather that everyone should have a change of mind toward His plan for the human race (2 Peter 3:9)—uses disaster to call the attention of the unsaved. In other words, God is saying to them through disaster, like He said to Saul en route to Damascus (Acts 9:1-5), "May I have your attention?" Usually, when one motions for attention, take for example in a social gathering, everyone stops and listens. Similarly, disasters such as cyclones, Hurricane Katrina, 9/11, earthquakes, unusual droughts, floods, tornadoes, and scorching heat, just to name a few, are all God's warning bells to get our attention! God is saying, "May I have your attention?"

Second, God uses disaster to compel carnal believers to get back on spiritual track. This we see from the confession of the Psalmist: "*Before I was afflicted I went astray, But now I keep Your word...It is good for me that I was afflicted, That I may learn Your statutes*" (Psalm 119:67-71). Excruciating pain forced the Psalmist back to God! Israel's experience throughout its history was a perfect example of this concept, as we saw in chapter 9.

What goes into our minds comes out in our actions. When we cease to saturate our souls with the divine viewpoint, we subscribe to the human viewpoint, which is demonic at best. Sooner or later, God will call our attention through disaster, as He did to Israel: "*In those times there was no peace to him who went out or to him who came in, for many disturbances afflicted all the inhabitants of the lands*" (2 Chronicles 15:5). Does that sound familiar to you? God inflicted them with mental pain and anguish according to His injunction (Deuteronomy 28:15-30). "*In their distress they turned to the LORD God*" (2 Chronicles 15:4).

Third, disaster is often God's way of helping spiritually minded believers develop spiritual capacity for extraordinary blessing (James 1:2-4). This we saw in the life of Job.

The challenging question is, how can we accurately decipher and classify disasters in our lives? The answer is simple:

self-examination (2 Corinthians 13:5)! That's right! Reflection (Haggai 1:5)! God will not give us a warning sign and leave us clueless as to what the sign is all about. God, in His grace, has given us the ability to decipher our experiences. The problem with us is often denial. God always leaves us with enough dots, but how often we tragically fail the simple test of connecting those dots! Many a times distraction become our worst enemy. It robs us the time and concentration needed for reflection.

On top of all this, by nature we are prone not to forget ill-treatment by others. We can trace the date, the time, and the exact place where someone wronged us. How good we are in connecting dots of our awkward experiences with other people! Some of us have such profound memories that we can connect the dots of our bad experiences all the way back to childhood. On the other hand, how quickly we develop the disease of amnesia when it comes to remembering when, where, and how we sowed a seed and the type of seed we sowed when harvest time comes. I think that the real issue with us is laziness. We become mentally lazy when it comes to connecting the past with the present. That ought to be conquered if we aspire to reap superabundant blessing, both in time and eternity! Scripture is so clear on the law of harvest: *"Do not be deceived, God is not mocked; for whatever a man sows, this he will also reap. For the one who sows to his own flesh shall from the flesh reap corruption [destruction], but the one who sows to the Spirit shall from the Spirit reap eternal life [blessing]"* (Galatians 6:7-8). That's to say, there's a direct link between our work and payday. We shouldn't have a difficult time interpreting disasters in our lives if we are sowing seeds of evil (Hosea 8:7). We shouldn't have a hard time deciphering our difficult circumstances if our spiritual life is in disarray (Hebrews 12:6). The truth remains, when we sow disobedience, we shall harvest disaster! When we sow seed of disregard to God's Word as a nation, sooner or later we shall reap every form of disaster.

We shall offer three examples to help drive our lesson home: postexilic Judah, Jacob, and my personal experience. With much said, we are poised to examine the correlation between the seed we sow and our fruit basket thereof. We begin with the postexilic Judah.

POSTEXILIC JUDAH

We saw briefly in chapter 9 Judah's colossal spiritual quagmire, which begged for divine discipline, that lasted for seventy years in Babylonian captivity according to God's Word (2 Chronicles 36:15-21). God in His grace, in faithfulness to His Word, orchestrated her return to Jerusalem when the time of His discipline was over (2 Chronicles 36:21-23; Jeremiah 25:11-12). How did God do that? God stirred up King Cyrus, who issued a decree in 538 B.C. in favor of the Jews, which allowed them to return to their land for a reconstruction project. That's sovereignty!

For one reason or another, the Jews abandoned the project God gave them when they returned, the temple's reconstruction. God's temple remained in shambles. They were busy rebuilding their own homes while ignoring the reconstruction project of God's temple that was in ruins during their Babylonian captivity. Rebuilding and furnishing their homes was more important to them than God's temple. They didn't care!

Our attitudes today reflect their attitudes! Many of us today don't care much about God's business. We don't care about missionary activities. They were busy with the construction of new homes; we find ourselves busy swimming in the pool of materialism. Same negligence, but in different form!

What do you think God would do in a situation like this? His justice will respond in kind. He responded then by sending drought throughout the land of Judah, and famine was the finale result (Haggai 1:11). That's great disaster in the land! To their amazement, everyone was in dismay and disbelief of how they could be in such bad shape agriculturally. They knew that it was the hand of God! Can we relate to their experience in any way?

God wanted them to solve the puzzle of their economic disaster; He wanted them to connect the dots: "*Then the word of the LORD came by Haggai the prophet, saying, 'Is it time for you yourselves to dwell in your [beautiful] paneled houses while this [temple] house lies desolate?' Now therefore, thus says the LORD of hosts, 'Consider your ways [reflect]!'*" (Haggai 1:3-5). Connect the dots! Solve the puzzle! God was saying there is a link between the concept that "*You have sown much, but harvest little; you eat, but there is not enough to be satisfied; you drink, but there is not enough to become drunk; you put on clothing, but no one is warm enough; and he who earns, earns wages to put into a purse with holes*" (Haggai 1:6). That's right! "*A purse with holes*"! God was draining their earnings! Who says that God cannot be involved in disaster!

"*Consider your ways!*" (Haggai 1:7)! Twice God called for reflection! In essence, God was telling them that there's always a connection between disobedience and disaster. "*I called for a drought on the land, on the mountains, on the grain, on the new wine, on the oil, on what the ground produces, on men, on cattle, and on all the labor of your hands*" (Haggai 1:11). My friend, you just read the Word of God. Question: who caused the drought? If we concur with

Scripture and say God, why then do we make an erroneous conclusion and blame a severe drought in California or Florida on so-called Mother Nature? We are reminded of the prophet's question, namely, when there is a disaster in a land, is the Lord not behind it? (Amos 3:6). God wants you and I to take the time, search our own lives and determine whether there is a connection between so many closed doors in our lives and our lifestyle. He wants us to isolate and categorize every disaster, one after another, and see whether there is a resemblance to the seed we are sowing or have sown in the past. Shall we do that?

As for the people of Judah, they did reflect. The result was that they had a change of mind and change of priorities. Rebuilding God's temple became foremost in their minds, and when they returned to God's project, God responded in kind with abundant blessing (Haggai 2:2-19). We read, "*Do consider from this day onward, from the twenty-fourth day of the ninth month [the day they returned to God's project]; from the day when the temple of the LORD was founded, consider*" (2:18). In essence, God was saying to His children, "From this day onward" "from this day you had a change of mind— from this day you had a change of priority—you will see the difference between blessing and cursing!" This brings us to Jacob's seed of deceit.

JACOB'S SEED OF DECEIT

God has spoken! Whatever a man sows, that he will reap in time of harvest! We are not unaware of Jacob's deceit, how he deceived his father Isaac and pretended to be his brother Esau and deceitfully stole his brother's blessing from their father Isaac (Genesis 27). His deception caused a rift between him and his brother Esau, which caused Jacob to run away from home. But before then he had already planted a seed of deception!

The first harvest came unexpectedly. While in the house of Laban, he fell in love with Rachel, the younger sister of Leah. Subsequently he asked Laban what the bride price would be. The would-be father-in-law told him to serve him for seven years. Because of his love, the Bible tells us that seven years seemed to Jacob but a few days (Genesis 29:20).

Seven years later Jacob could hardly wait for the marriage deal to be ratified!

> Then Jacob said to Laban, "Give me my wife, for my time is completed, that I may go in to her." Laban gathered all the men of the place and made a feast. Now in the evening he[secretly] took his daughter Leah, and brought her to him [in the dark]; and Jacob went in to her [thinking that he had slept with his true love]. Laban also gave his maid Zilpah to his daughter Leah as a maid. So it came about in the morning that, behold, it was Leah! And he said to Laban, "What is this you have done to me? Was it not for Rachel that I served with you? Why then have you deceived me?" (Genesis 29:21-25).

Jacob actually asked, "Why then have you deceived me?" How quickly he obliterated from his mind that he recently sowed the seed of deception in his father's vineyard when he wore goat skins to make his skin feel like that of Esau (Genesis 27:16-23)! The truth of the matter is that no one eludes the law of harvest: "Do not be deceived, God is not mocked; for whatever a man sows, this he will also reap. For the one who sows to his own flesh shall from the flesh reap corruption [destruction], but the one who sows to the Spirit shall from the

Spirit reap eternal life [blessing]" (Galatians 6:7-8). Twenty years later, his own children brought him another fruit basket of deception when they sold his beloved son Joseph and brought back his multi-colored tunic, which they soiled in a pool of animal's blood.[72]

> *And they sent the varicolored tunic and brought it to their father and said, "We found this; please examine it to see whether it is your son's tunic or not." Then he examined it and said, "It is my son's tunic. A wild beast has devoured him; Joseph has surely been torn to pieces!" So Jacob tore his clothes, and put sackcloth on his loins and mourned for his son many days* (Genesis 37:32-34).

My friend, God can never go back on His Word! When we sow to the wind, we shall ultimately reap a hurricane in time of harvest (Hosea 8:7). Such is the law of harvest!

This brings us to the next example, which I am somewhat hesitant to write about. This is because it's personal and very humbling. We shall save it for the last, but before then, let's consider self-examination.

SELF-EXAMINATION

King Solomon, the wisest man who ever lived, through the ministry of the Holy Spirit exhorted us, saying, "*In the day of prosperity be happy, But in the day of adversity [disaster] consider [reflect]—God has made the one [blessing] as well as the other [disaster]*" (Ecclesiastes 7:14). The main point in Solomon's exhortation is reflection. He does not want us to take blessing and disaster in our lives for granted. He wants us to reflect!

---

72 Moses C. Onwubiko, *Joseph, a Pillar of Grace.*

Self-examination requires maximum concentration. It requires that we rid ourselves of every distraction that may interfere with our concentration in connecting the dots with regard to our spiritual life and present suffering. It requires that our minds be in a state whereby we can see clearly in our souls the searchlight of God the Holy Spirit as He shows us every seed-like dot in our souls. In the heat of the moment, we make King David's cry our own: "*Search me, O God, and know my heart; Try me and know my anxious thoughts; And see if there be any hurtful way in me, And lead me in the everlasting way*" (Psalm 139:23-24, cf. 77:6; 4:4). "*Let the words of my mouth and the meditation of my heart Be acceptable in Your sight, O LORD, my rock and my Redeemer*" (Psalm 19:14).

One may ask, "What are the mechanisms of reflection?" This question brings us face-to-face with the self-examination mechanism, which will underscore the connection between the seed of disobedience or evil behavior and disaster.

SELF-EXAMINATION MECHANISM

In this mind exercise, you are to take a long hard vacation in your soul and apply the principle of reflection. Recall that reflection is an act of soul retreat, whereby one intensively searches one's soul and retraces one's ways of life and past actions in light of cause and effect. You have the option of using your mind or a piece of paper in this exercise of dot-connection. The following steps are suggested:

Step One

The first and foremost step is to deal with the real issue in life, namely your spiritual life. You should ask yourself a series of personal questions, such as, how is my spiritual life?

How serious am I both in the intake of God's Word and its application? We should be very careful not to misconstrue attending Bible class on a regularly basis and accumulating spiritual knowledge as actually living the spiritual life. Self-deception overtakes us if we are regular attendees of Bible class but are worse than unbelievers in our manner of life. Remember the words of the apostle Paul:

> *But realize this, that in the last days difficult times will come. For men will be lovers of self, lovers of money, boastful, arrogant, revilers, disobedient to parents, ungrateful, unholy, unloving, irreconcilable, malicious gossips, without self-control, brutal, haters of good, treacherous, reckless, conceited, lovers of pleasure rather than lovers of God, holding to a form of godliness, although they have denied its power; Avoid such men as these. For among them are those who enter into house-holds and captivate weak women weighed down with sins, led on by various impulses,* **always learning and never able to come to the [point of actually applying the] truth** (2 Timothy 3:1-7, emphasis added).

Step Two

The next question you should ask yourself is this: "Am I resisting God's directive will for my life?" In other words, is there anything the Lord is directing me to do in life that I am opposing outright? Does God want me to serve Him in the ministry or go somewhere and I am resisting with all my might? Again, these questions should be answered soberly. Recall that God used disaster to get Jonah to comply with God's will for his life (Jonah 1-3:1).

With step one and two settled, you come to the last step.

Step Three

The third thing you need to do is to carefully evaluate the nature of your disaster, whether it has to do with bad judgment on your part. But if your judgment had no bearing on it, then you can narrow it to one of two conclusions. 1. God in His matchless grace is sending you a warning signal to reverse your rebellious or carnal course before it's too late (Hebrews 12:6; Proverbs 29:1). 2. God in His infinite wisdom is using the disaster to enhance your ongoing spiritual life in order to position you for supreme blessing (Job 23:10; cf. James 1:2-4,12; Romans 8:28). If so, after the examination, you will discover that your spiritual life is sound.

The truth is, when we are honest to ourselves in our reflection, the interpretation of our dilemma becomes much easier. When we are honest and respond to God's warning signal through acknowledgment of our failures (1 John 1:9) and adjustment to His plan accordingly, God in His unfathomable grace will respond in kind. The prophet Isaiah beckons us to "*Seek the LORD while He may be found; Call upon Him while He is near. Let the wicked forsake his Way And the unrighteous man his thoughts; And let him return to the LORD, And He will have compassion on him, And to our God, For He will abundantly pardon*" (Isaiah 55:6-7). That's grace! With this in mind, we can now proceed to the last illustration of the law of harvest—the law of sowing and reaping, my personal experience.

Resisting God's Will

The apostle Paul asked whether anyone has been successful in resisting God's will (Romans 9:19). Make no mistake: when God speaks, that's *final*! That means all human debates and roundtable discussions must come to adjournment. Snow, rain, sunshine, pull, push, or drag, the will of God will be done! We pay an avoidable costly price when we resist His will. That was the case with Balaam, who wanted to curse Israel, contrary to God's will (Numbers 22:12). He set forth to go against the will of God; consequently he paid dearly (Numbers 22:13-23:26). That's true for Jonah, whom the Lord asked to go to Nineveh. He chose to go against God's will and paid a costly price too (Jonah 1:1-17). There's no getting around God's will. In a nutshell, that's the meaning of God's sovereignty!

I learned that lesson the hard way. The truth of the matter is that God often uses closed doors, hardship, and disaster, one after another, to force us to comply with His will. Sovereignty always wins. No matter what!

I grew up in a small village called Amaba, in the southeastern part of Nigeria, a country that sits on the west coast of Africa. Born into a family that practiced occultism, I was locked up in ignorance of the True God until God graciously opened my eyes through a group who brought His gospel message to our village. There and then, the Holy Spirit bestowed on me the spiritual gift of communication. I was still in the third grade when I trusted in Christ and broke away from the religious bondage that held our family for so long. As my parents and siblings were exposed to the gospel, they too responded by faith alone in Christ alone.

My spiritual gift became obvious to everyone around. On fire for the gospel, while still in elementary school I began preaching in churches, trains, buses, schools, and villages. I knew what my spiritual gift was, and so did many pastors and villagers, who heard me give the gospel on many occasions. They too reached the same conclusion.

Amazingly, as part of God's plan for my life, through my eldest brother, Dr. C. Onwubiko (whose own testimony of his encounter with God is intriguing), God brought me to the United States of America leaving my other siblings behind in Nigeria. Simply, were it not for God's grace, everything stood against me having any chance of coming to the United States. Two decades later, my elders are only dreaming about this great country! The thought still fills me with humility within. But that's not all!

When I came to this country of awesome opportunity, I had a dual ambition, namely, attending seminary and becoming a neurosurgeon. The former was God's plan while the latter was mine. Seeing that God had blessed me with academic prowess, I pursued my medical ambition, at the expense of His will for my life. Another Jonah?

To summarize the story, God pursued me with love, compassion, grace, and discipline as I pursued my medical career. On the one hand, God's will was for me to be in the ministry. On the other hand, my goal was to be in a surgery room. What would it take to resolve this conflict? Take a guess. That's right! Disaster!

Solomon tells us that foolishness is bound in the heart of every child and that only the rod of discipline can drive stubbornness away (Proverbs 22:15). This is true of us all!

Disaster is usually a-God-orchestrated messenger to get our attention (2 Chronicles 15:2-6). We read the words of the Psalmist afresh: "*Before I was afflicted I went astray [like many of us are today], But now I keep Your word...It is good for me that I was afflicted, that I may learn Your statutes*" (Psalm 119:67-71).

The author of the book of Hebrews casts a beam of light on the concept of discipline, saying,

> *"For those whom the Lord loves He disciplines, and He scourges every son whom He receives." It is for discipline that you endure; God deals with you as with sons; for what son is there whom his father does not discipline? But if you are without discipline, of which all have become partakers, then you are illegitimate children and not sons. Furthermore, we had earthly fathers to discipline us, and we respected them; shall we not much rather be subject to the Father of spirits, and live? For they [our earthly parents] disciplined us for a short time as seemed best to them, but He [God] disciplines us for our good, that we may share His holiness. All discipline for the moment seems not to be joyful, but sorrowful; yet to those who have been trained by it, afterwards it yields the peaceful fruit of righteousness* (Hebrews 12:6-11).

There we have it on record, the manifestation of both the love of God and His justice. Discipline is a stilled voice of grace that we all need to heed (Proverbs 3:11). Like the author of Hebrews points out, it's the parental expression of love to their children. He underscores that *"All discipline for the moment seems not to be joyful, but sorrowful; yet to those who have been trained by it, afterwards it yields the peaceful fruit of righteousness."* What a true statement!

God, in His infinite love, grace, and justice, orchestrated disaster, one after another, as warning bells to force me to reflect and yield to His plan for my life. First, He hit me with an unusual headache that kept threatening my career, a headache that baffled even the best-of-the-best neurologists.

I knew it was the hand of God and yet forged along in my career amidst my indescribable pain. Then God took me through a series of car wrecks. I had eight close-call accidents within ten years or so. In my reflections, it was clear to me that God was sending me warning bells. But as soon as I recovered, I got a new car. if my car was totaled, I would turn my ears off from the warning bells. In addition, God closed every door airtight!

For thirteen years I was in resistance mode. On many occasions, my wife asked me, "Are we experiencing divine discipline or something else?" I said to her, "Oh no, something else, of course! We are learning the Word of God every day, and so what we are going through cannot be a discipline." But deep in my soul, I knew we were in trouble with the supreme court of Heaven! She knew that too! She even suggested that I abandon everything and pursue my calling in life, which she too was convinced about. I brushed her idea off in a hurry!

But one evening, when I was returning from work, the final warning bell came. I had a head-on collision with a drunk driver. My car was totaled beyond recognition! My wife had cold feet when she saw the car at the towing garage. The man who showed us the car was in disbelief when I told him that I was the driver of the car. Simply, God graced me out! On the other hand, I saw how close I came to being six feet under.

I called my brother from the hospital around midnight. The first words that came out of my mouth, before I told him where I was and why I was calling him that late, were "God still has a plan for my life." My friend, that did it for me! The wresting game was over. Pull, push or drag, God will win! He won!

I had a change of mind and a change of direction similar to the experience of the postexilic-Judah in Haggai's day. Because of their change of mind toward the plan of God, as we have already noted, the Lord promised them a super-abundance of blessing (Haggai 1:14-15; 2:15-19). As the Lord would have it, in 1997, He used me as a vessel to establish Grace Evangelistic Ministries, a ministry that He has blessed abundantly.

Guess what? God, in His unfathomable grace, also took care of those frequent accidents and mysterious headache. Ever since then, I have not had any CT scans done on my brain; nor have I been involved in any accident. Much more: God, in His infinite mercy, has showered us with blessings, in many ways totally beyond our imaginations. In twelve years and counting, my wife has never asked those repeated questions that she used to ask when I was in defiance of God's will for my life. Rather, she glories in the Lord! This does not mean that we are free from suffering, however. On the contrary, we experience a different kind of suffering in varying degrees, as our Lord promised every believer (John 16:33; cf. Philippians 1:29), but with peace and joy (James 1:2; cf. Galatians 5:22). That's the difference!

What's more, God has through this ministry shown mercy to many including Muslim and Hindu people around the world. Many have come to the saving knowledge of our Lord and Savior Jesus Christ. You, too, can trust in Him and experience peace, if you have not already done so. Again, that's God's grace in action. What redemption there is when we respond to a disaster in our lives that's tailored as a warning bell! I learned this lesson the hard way with many bruises, but you don't have to go that route. You don't have to wait until it's too late. Reflect! His grace abounds!

"*Seek the LORD while He may be found; Call upon Him while He is near. Let the wicked forsake his Way And the unrighteous man his thoughts; And let him return to the LORD, And He will have compassion on him, And to our God, For He will abundantly pardon*" (Isaiah 55:6-7). "*In the day of prosperity be happy, But in the day of adversity [disaster] consider [reflect]—God has made the one [blessing] as well as the other [disaster]*" (Ecclesiastes 7:14).

I would like to conclude this section and our work in general with a portion of a letter that my friend, as well as a partner on the frontline of the gospel, John G. Brunner, wrote to his friends and associates during a Memorial Day weekend:

> But all is not well in our country. We are facing serious problems at home, as well as overseas. I really believe that, as individuals, we have drifted off course and are heading to the rock and coral reefs that will risk our ship of state. I am reminded of the following quote that seems to sum up the dreadful cycle of every civilization…Clarence Manion, the dean of the Notre Dame Law School from 1941-1952, boarded a plane sometime during the 1950s. One of the passengers recognized him and went over and sat down next to him. Dean Manion was doing some work, but he had to put it all away as this man began asking questions. He wanted to talk with the professor about the unfortunate condition of our country. Dean Manion listened patiently, conversed with him, and began making notes while the man was speaking. As the plane landed he got up, shook hands with the man…and handed him a slip of paper on which he had written these words:

Man begins his existence in bondage,
and rises from bondage through spiritual faith,
from spiritual faith to courage,
from courage to liberty
from liberty to abundance
from abundance to selfishness,
from selfishness to complacency,
from complacency to apathy,
from apathy to dependence,
from dependence back to bondage.

We are challenged by the prophets of old: "[If] *My people who are called by My name humble themselves and pray and seek My face and turn from their wicked ways, then I will hear from heaven, will forgive their sin and will heal their land*" (2 Chronicles 7:14). Therefore, we are forced to conclude that the divine solution is the only recourse for any person or nation that is under divine discipline because of disregard to the laws of divine establishment.

Before you put this book down, I would like for you to meditate on His Word: "*Seek the LORD while He may be found; Call upon Him while He is near. Let the wicked forsake his way and the unrighteous man his thoughts; And let him return to the LORD, And He will have compassion on him, And to our God, For He will abundantly pardon*" (Isaiah 55:6-7).

It's my heartfelt prayer that God, in His infinite mercy, would open our eyes, so that we may realize that we are just a couple of steps away from falling off a cliff. May He cause every one of us in this nation and around the world to reflect on our spiritual lives and amend our ways in a hurry! May we take advantage of our God, who is full of loving-kindness, compassion and mercy, and return to Him. May the content of this book bring much needed revival and blessing in our lives. It's my humble prayer that the God of revival would revive us according to the riches of His grace in Christ Jesus. May He grant us our hearts' desires as we seek Him with all our hearts. This I pray in the Name of the King of kings, Lord of lords, our Wonderful Savior, Jesus Christ. Amen!

Now to Him who is able to do far more abundantly beyond all that we ask or think, according to the power that works within us, to Him be the glory in the church and in Christ Jesus to all generations forever and ever. Amen (Ephesians 3:20-21).

Bibliography

Blankley, Tony. *The West's Last Chance: Will We Win the Clash of Civilization?* Washington, DC: Regnery Publishing Inc., 2005.

Enns, Paul. *The Moody Handbook of Theology.* Chicago: Moody Press, 1989.

Federer, William J. *America's God and Country, Encyclopedia of Quotations.* St Louis, Mo: Amerisearch, Inc., 2000.

Gaebelein, Frank E. *The Expositors Bible Commentary,* volume 8 with the New International Version. Grand Rapids: Zondervan, 1984.

Gibbon, Edward. *The Decline and Fall of the Roman Empire* (An Abridgment by D. M. Low). New York: Harcourt, Brace and Company, 1960.

Ironside, H. A. *Philippians.* Baltimore, Maryland: Loizeaux, 1997.

Kirk, Russell. *The Roots of American Order.* Washington, DC: Regnery Gateway, 1991.

La Sor, William Sanford, David Allan Hubbard, Frederic William Bush, and Leslie C. Allen. *Old Testament*

Survey. Grand Rapids: Eerdmans Publishing Company, 1982.

Lewis, Gordon R. "God, Attributes of." *Evangelical Dictionary of Theology*. Walter A Elwell, ed. Grand Rapids: Baker 1984.

Orr, James. *The International Standard Bible Encyclopaedia* (volume III). Grand Rapids: Eerdmans, 1956.

Schaeffer, Frances A. *How Should We Then Live? The Rise and Decline of Western Thought and Culture*. Wheaton, Illinois: Crossway Books, 2005.

Schweikart, Larry, and Michael Allen. *A Patriot's History of the United States from Columbus Great Discovery to the War on Terror*. New York: Penguin Group, 2004.

Singer, C. Gregg. *A Theological Interpretation of American History*. Greenville, South Carolina: A Press, 1994.

Thiessen, Henry C. *Lectures in Systematic Theology*. Grand Rapids: Eerdmans, 1977.

Tuchman, Barbara W. *Bible and Sword: England and Palestine from the Bronze Age to Balfour*. New York: Ballantine Books, 1956.

Vine, W. E., and Merrill F. Unger. *Vine's Complete Expository Dictionary of Old and New Testament Words*. Nashville: Thomas Nelson Publishing, 1996.

Warfield, B. B. "Trinity." *The International Standard Bible Encyclopedia*. James Orr, ed. Grand Rapids: Eerdmans, 1930.

Willmington, H. L. *Willmington's Guide to the Bible*. Wheaton, Illinois: Tyndale House Publishers, Inc., 1984.

Publications Available Free of Charge

Riding the Death Train
(A powerful tool for evangelism)

Montados en el Tren de la Muerte
(Riding the Death Train in Spanish)

Eternal Security of the Believer

Comfort in Suffering

God's Plan after Salvation

Biblical Doctrine of Salvation

Focus on Christian Marriage

Overview of God's Grace

Paul, a Trophy of God's Grace

Joseph, A Pillar of Grace

Signs & Wonders (A Biblical Reply to the Claims of
Modern Day Miracle Workers)

The Spiritual Gift of Tongues (A Biblical Response to
Modern Day Tongues)

Disaster: God's Warning Bell

Grow in the grace and knowledge of our Lord and
Savior Jesus Christ. To Him be the glory, both now and
To the day of eternity. Amen (2 Peter 3:18).

To receive this or any other publication,
please write:

In the U.S.A.
Grace Evangelistic Ministries
P. O. Box 111999
Nashville, TN 37222-1999
U.S.A.

In Africa
Grace Evangelistic Ministries
P. O. Box 583
Jos, Plateau State
Nigeria
www.Gemworldwide.org